THE PAIN AND THE JOY
Reflections on the Spiritual Life

by
Edward Carter, S.J.

Published by:
Faith Publishing Company
P.O. Box 237
Milford, Ohio 45150

IMPRIMI POTEST: Robert A. Wild, S.J.

IMPRIMATUR: Most Rev. James H. Garland
Auxiliary Bishop
Archdiocese of Cincinnati

Published by: Faith Publishing Company
P.O. Box 237
Milford, OH 45150

For additional copies address Faith Publishing Company

ACKNOWLEDGMENTS:

Scripture texts used in this work are taken from THE NEW AMERICAN BIBLE WITH REVISED NEW TESTAMENT, c 1986, by the Confraternity of Christian Doctrine, Washington, D.C., and are used by permission of the copyright owner. All rights reserved.

Cover design by Pete Massari, Rockford, IL.

Copyright, 1992: Edward Carter, S.J.

Library of Congress Catalog Card No.: 92-75485

ISBN No.: 1-880033-05-4

Table of Contents

Publisher's Foreword

It is a troubled world we live in. The simple life style seems to be a thing of the past, and we are faced with complex issues that require our discernment even in our day to day activities. Our culture seems to be built around controversy, materialism, greed and a humanism that has somehow replaced the Creator in favor of the creature. There is an urgent need to adjust our focus.

Here is a book that goes a long way toward achieving that goal. Fr. Edward Carter offers a series of reflections, or meditations, that can contribute greatly in helping us to get our priorities back in line. These reflections on the spiritual aspect of our lives, our persons, are based on reaching a better understanding of the attributes of our inner self, and what is needed to round out that image of a well balanced, responsible, and satisfied Christian in today's world. Here is a book that spells out the criteria for developing that day to day relationship with Jesus Christ.

In reviewing Fr. Carter's work here, it is worthwhile to point out that this book should have a place in the library of every Christian reader. It is not a book that focuses on only Catholic teaching, but on the teaching of Christ as it has been handed down to all believers.

vi   *The Pain and the Joy*

Assuredly, if all Christians could apply the principles presented in this book to their personal lives, it would go a long way toward creating that peaceful and unified world we all speak of, but which appears to be so far off on the horizon.

We encourage you to consider not reading this book on a "from cover-to-cover" basis, but instead, browse through the table of contents and select one topic at a time to read and ponder. With the grace of the Holy Spirit, you will frequently be led to a wonderful essay which not only speaks to your heart, but may also draw you into an easier, more intimate, comfortable friendship with Jesus.

Fr. Edward Carter is a Jesuit priest who holds a doctorate in theology. He is a professor of theology at Xavier University in Cincinnati and his concentration is in spirituality. Along these lines he has authored a dozen books on this topic including: *Response in Christ, The Mysticism of Everyday, Prayer Perspectives, The Jesus Experience,* and *Response to God's Love.* We applaud his commitment to helping build a better world through his printed word.

FAITH PUBLISHING COMPANY

Preface

We have a reflective, contemplative dimension to our persons. We must allow this aspect of our beings to have proper expression and nourishment if we are to grow properly. We of industrialized cultures consistently must remind ourselves of this truth. Our cultures place heavy emphasis upon the external order of things—being externally active, getting things done with due dispatch. In such a climate our innate desire for reflection can be all but completely stifled unless we are adamant in our determination not to allow such a loss to occur.

This book of short reflections is an attempt to aid today's Christian in giving proper attention to the contemplative aspect of one's person. In compiling this set of reflections, I have drawn from works on the spiritual life which I have previously published, while at the same time I have added new material. In other books I have given a more extended development of spiritual themes, while in the present work I offer, for the most part, fewer ideas concerning the various topics. There is, obviously, a place for both approaches. Sometimes we desire a more extended treatment of spiritual themes; at other times we wish to have merely a few ideas on a greater variety of topics.

The book can be used in a number of ways. One can use it for spiritual reading. One can also use it as an aid for reflection and prayer. It can also be a source of ideas for groups of people engaged in shared prayer. Finally, I am hopeful that it may be of aid to those who give homilies and talks on the spiritual life.

Edward Carter, S.J.
Xavier University

1

Jesus and the Christian

We are currently witnessing a resurgence of interest in popular psychology. Psychology books for popular audiences have flooded the market in recent years. Of course, this proliferation of psychological literature is commensurate with readers' demands for such material, and such, signifies that there are numerous individuals interested in a more complete understanding of the workings of the human psyche. People want to learn how to cope more successfully with emotional problems, how to relate with others in a more mature and satisfying fashion, how to develop into fulfilled individuals.

As contemporary Christians, we are obviously exposed to the influence of these publications, but we must take a balanced attitude toward this literature. On the one hand, we realize that psychology can certainly tell us much that is true and helpful concerning the behavior of the human person. On the other hand, we should realize that a certain portion of psychological literature is either indifferent or even hostile toward religion.

Even when we assimilate what is good from psychology concerning the human person and human behavior, we must still realize we do not possess the entire truth regarding the human personality. As Christians, however, we do

1

have a source which gives us the ultimate truth concerning what it means to be human. This source is Christ Himself; Jesus is the supreme personality theorist. He is the one, who, by His teaching and example, tells us what human life is really all about, how we must think and act if we are to satisfy that consistent yearning for fulfillment and happiness which is etched deeply within the human heart.

Jesus leads us to personality fulfillment, not by removing us from the human condition, but by teaching us how properly to live within it. Sometimes we are tempted to think that the best way to be a good Christian would be to withdraw as much as possible from earthly concerns. We think how peaceful it would be to dwell alone with God in our own kind of hermitage, and allow the world with all its worries, anxieties, and temptations to pass us by. In moments of clear reflection, however, we realize this is an unrealistic kind of thinking, thinking which does not correspond to Christ's redemptive plan (indeed, even the cloistered contemplative must properly encounter the human situation).

Jesus redeemed us within the framework of the human condition. Jesus' enfleshment placed Him within the world of the human, and He accepted the implications of His manhood. He lived His humanity to the fullest by always doing His Father's will with love. He lived a full human life not only when it was pleasant to do so, but also when this meant being nailed to a cross in excruciating agony.

All of Jesus' human acts contributed to His redemptive effort: His relationships with Mary, Joseph, and others; His taking meals with friends; His gathering the little children to Himself in warm embrace; His healing of the sick; His thrilling to nature's beauty; the sufferings of

His passion and death. Yes, these and all His other human acts redeemed us.

As Jesus objectively redeemed us within the framework of the human condition, so in like manner we subjectively participate in redemption. We live the life Jesus came to give by experiencing humanity according to God's will. We are saved, not by fleeing from it, but by embracing it according to God's designs.

As Jesus did before us, we also must accept the human experience not only at those times when life rewards us with joy, success, enthusiasm, and the beauty and tenderness of life. When we experience failure or misunderstanding, when we taste the bitterness of human existence, when life seems all too much for us, when anguish and intense suffering make even one day seem endless—at these times also we must affirm our being human. In this way we are saved. In this way we help others be saved. In this way we follow Jesus, who is both God and man.

If we are to live the human condition properly, we must live it according to the vision of Christ. Indeed, Jesus came to give us a new vision. As we are drawn into the Jesus experience by God's merciful love, we are graced with a new way of looking at things. We must allow this vision to consistently shape the way we view persons, places, things, and events.

It is not always easy to live according to the vision of Christ. There is much in the world which is opposed to the teaching of Jesus. If we do not take the proper precautions, the false views of the world can gradually blur the vision Jesus has granted us.

A worldly false view, for instance, tells us that we are successful only if we are successful in the external order of things. Christ's view tells us that we are really successful only if we live according to His Father's will.

A worldly false view tells us that the more material things we possess, the more fortunate we are. Christ's view tells us that material things are worthwhile in proportion to their helping us live the life He came to give us, and that we must exercise a constant vigilance lest material possessions become an end in themselves rather than a legitimate means to a noble goal.

A worldly false view presents a hedonistic pursuit of pleasure and an avoidance of suffering at all costs as an ideal to be pursued. Christ's view assigns pleasure its legitimate place within God's plan for human existence, but simultaneously reminds us that suffering is also a part of the human condition, and we must take up our cross daily and follow Him.

A worldly view uses others in a manipulative fashion, telling those who would listen, to use others for the attainment of selfish goals. Christ's view reminds us that each person is made in the image of God, possesses a priceless dignity, and should be loved accordingly.

A worldly view has no time for meditation and contemplation, considering such exercises a waste of time—the occupation of pious individuals who lack the shrewdness and toughness to accomplish successfully in the arena of worldly competition. Christ's view persistently reminds us that prayerful communication with our transcendent God is necessary for a truly human existence.

Christ's view of reality must affect not only the intellectual aspect of our being, but must permeate our entire persons, if indeed we are to be mature Christian personalities. In this regard we can make a distinction between a notional assent and an existential assent regarding our acceptance of Christ's vision. With a merely notional assent our intellects do indeed accept Christ's truth. But this notional assent does not influence our entire persons in a consistent, dynamic fashion. We believe in Christ and His teaching, but there are numerous areas of our existence which do not, in a consistent fashion, come under the influence of Christ's truth.

With an existential assent, on the other hand, we assent to the truth of Christ, not merely in the intellectual dimension of our personalities, but with our entire being. Through a proper asceticism and a life of meditation and contemplation, we allow the truth of Christ to more and more penetrate through the ugly layers of the errant self to the vibrant realms of the true self in the center of our personalities. This existential assent to the truth of Christ, is what allows our true personalities to emerge and to influence what we think, say, and do. Faith, hope, and love more and more exercise their purgative, illuminative, and transforming effects upon our personalities, and, consequently, the words of St. Paul increasingly have meaning for us:

> . . .*yet I live, no longer I, but Christ lives in me; insofar as I now live in the flesh, I live by faith in the Son of God who has loved me and given himself up for me.* (*Gal.* 2:20).

As Christians then, we are called to transformation in Christ. This obviously entails a friendship with Jesus, one which becomes increasingly close.

Friendship is a process of self-liberation. As I give myself to another in friendship, I am aided in the process of escape from my false self. I am aided in the process of achieving true self-identity. The facade of the false self more and more recedes through the dynamics of friendship. Why is this? When another receives me in friend-

ship, that other receives me as I am. The friend loves me
in my good points, loves me despite my bad points. In the
warmth of this receptive love, I am encouraged to be and
to become my authentic self. I do not have to project a false
self in the hope that such an image might be more acceptable to the other. Rather, I am encouraged to take the risk
of being my true self, since I know the other will not reject
me. Actually, my true self is more attractive to the friend
and to others precisely because it is my authentic self—the
self God destines me to be, possessing the personal
uniqueness with which God has permeated my being.

  Friendship, therefore, increases my freedom—the freedom to be my real self. The deeper an authentic friendship, the more I am encouraged by the other's love to be
and to become. I am encouraged to exercise my talents
and to develop them to ever greater heights in the loving
service of God and others.
  If friendship with a human person increases my
growth potential, what are we to say about friendship
with Jesus? There is no comparison. Jesus offers me such
magnificent opportunities for growth. The more I am
aware of Jesus' tremendous and personal love for me, the
more secure I feel in developing my real self.

  Being accepted by Jesus as a friend should radically
change my life. As Jesus has given Himself entirely to me,
so I should give myself entirely to Him. This deep and
intense friendship accomplishes my ongoing conversion,
my transformation. This friend Jesus, through the strength
and tenderness of His love, gradually and increasingly
draws me out of my selfish traits. He gradually makes me
freer to really be. He increasingly assists me in allowing
my Christic, Trinitarian self to emerge more and more in
expressions of love for God and neighbor.

As I share the pleasant experiences of life with this friend Jesus, He enhances their joy. Being loved and accepted by others, enjoying the challenge and success of work, experiencing simple joys as well as moments of overwhelming happiness, drinking in the breathless beauties of nature—these and all such experiences take on deeper meaning in the presence of Jesus.

As I share the difficult aspects of human life with Jesus, He lessens their burden. If Jesus is my friend, should I ever capitulate to discouragement. If Jesus is my friend, should a sense of failure ever extinguish my determination to struggle on? If Jesus is my friend, is there any cross I can claim is too heavy? If Jesus is my friend, can I ever allow suffering to make me bitter?

As I strive to grow into a mature Christian, this friend Jesus is profoundly present to me. He is strong, tender, understanding, gentle, loving. He sympathizes, encourages, challenges, inspires. He leads, but does not force. He admonishes us when we are wrong, but He does not reject us. He is overjoyed at our good deeds, yet gently but firmly reminds us that there is still much to accomplish as He guides us in the Spirit to the Father. Jesus is the perfect friend. He is your friend, and my friend.

An excellent way to grow in our relationship with Jesus is through devotion to His Sacred Heart. Christ shows us His Heart as symbol of His love. In His great love for us He asks for our love in return. Can we refuse? Can we refuse this Christ who, out of love for us, experienced the piercing of His Heart on a hill called Calvary? Christ gave Himself entirely. Nailed to the wood of a cross, He poured out His life. Christ did this for love of us—for you, and for me.

As Jesus gives Himself so completely to us, it is entirely fitting that we make a return gift. It is entirely proper that we give ourselves, out of love, to Him. This total gift of self is called "consecration." Consecration to the Heart of Christ is the gift of ourselves and all of our faculties to Christ. We in effect say, "Jesus, take me whole and entire. Out of love I give myself entirely to You. Live in and through me. In love You have given Yourself completely to me. In love I give myself completely to You."

To aid us in living out our consecration to the Heart of Christ we should also consecrate ourselves to the Immaculate Heart of Mary. At Fatima Our Lady revealed that Jesus desires that devotion to the Immaculate Heart exist together with devotion to His own Heart. Our Lady of Fatima promised the great gift of salvation to all those who practice devotion to her Immaculate Heart. The highest form of such devotion is consecration to Mary the Immaculate Heart.

Through this consecration we give ourselves entirely to Mary so that she may lead us ever closer to the Heart of her Son. Consecration to the Immaculate Heart, then, is a great help in the living out of our consecration to the Heart of Christ in an ever progressive way.

All we shall say in the following pages has a relationship to living out this consecration to the Heart of Christ and to the Immaculate Heart of Mary. Christ and Mary— how much they love us! They reveal their Hearts as symbols of this love. They ask for our love in return. They invite us to live within their Hearts. If we accept their invitation, we experience love and peace despite the painful aspects of life. We experience security. We experience joy and happiness. Yes, Christ and Mary invite us to live within their Hearts in order that such a life may be ours. Who can refuse their invitation?

2

The Pain and the Joy

Certain people look upon religion as a type of enslavement. Religion, claim these people, puts shackles on one's desires for full living, pleasure, and happiness. Religion, they continue, makes you fearful, forces you into a rigid pattern of dos and don'ts which restricts and even suffocates your thrust toward full personality development. Whatever the causes may be for one's arriving at this view, such an attitude grossly misrepresents the nature of true religion.

Jesus has come to make us happy, not to make us participate in a religion which destroys the joy-dimension of human life. Jesus has come to increase our capacity for true self-fulfillment, not to restrict us with a religion which (while encouraging morbid self-enclosement), destroys possibilities for healthy self-expansion. Jesus has come to show us the way to true pleasure, not to present us with a religion which looks askance at such. Furthermore, this happiness and fulfillment which Jesus has come to give us is meant for this life as well as for eternal life. Christianity is a religion which gives a here-and-now happiness that develops into a future and eternal happiness. It satisfies our deepest desires to be fully

9

alive. Furthermore, Christianity is a religion which
unites pain and joy.

Christ's followers have looked upon His sufferings—
which culminated in the agony of Calvary—and have
been moved to a most unique kind of compassion; for
the sufferings of Jesus are those of the completely inno-
cent one, sufferings of an extremely kind, sensitive, and
loving man. Here was a man who had done nothing but
good, and yet, in the end He suffered rejection, betrayal,
and denial.

Nevertheless, this classical figure of suffering and
pathos who is Jesus is also the classical figure of hope.
The crucified Jesus is the great symbol of hope because
His suffering and death point beyond Calvary to His
Resurrection. The suffering and pathos of Jesus opens up
into hope-causing and joy-causing resurrection. The
Jesus who exacts compassion from His followers is the
same Jesus who fills them with resurrection joy, peace,
and happiness. Jesus allows the Christian to see that
suffering is not meant to be self-enclosed, but rather
open-ended. Suffering is meant, when properly assimilated, to lead to greater life, to greater love, joy, and
happiness.

The pain and the joy of life are inevitably linked
together. Let us not try to separate them. On the one
hand, let us not narrowly view life's suffering so that
we fail to see it as a means, if properly encountered, to
a fuller life. On the other hand, let us not so exclusively
focus on the aspect of joy that we fail to remember that
its presence in our life cannot be maintained and
deepened unless we are willing to suffer with Jesus. Pain
and joy—what God has joined together, let us not strive
to separate.

Dying and rising were inseparable in Jesus' existence.

Since we have been baptized into Christ's death-resurrection, as St. Paul tells us (*Rom.* 6:1-11), dying and rising are also inseparable in our own existence. The pain and the joy. In experiencing humanity, the Christian must assimilate both according to God's designs.

To Teach as Jesus Taught.

3

Mother at Our Side

In the Gospel of John we read words which should always be a source of great consolation for us:

> Standing by the cross of Jesus were his mother and his mother's sister, Mary the wife of Clopas, and Mary of Magdala. When Jesus saw his mother and the disciple there whom he loved, he said to his mother, 'Woman, behold, your son.' Then he said to the disciple, 'Behold, your mother.' (Jn. 19:25-27).

In giving Mary to the disciple, Jesus has also given her to each of us. Behold, then, one of God's greatest gifts to us—Mary as our spiritual mother.

As Mary cooperated with the Holy Spirit in first giving Christ to the world, so she continues to work with the Spirit in giving Jesus to each of us. Under God, Mary gives us our life of grace, our Christ-life. With her maternal love she protects and nourishes this life. Mary's desire for us is that we continue to grow in Christ, that increasingly we experience transformation in Him. Her overwhelming love for us, then, is evident.

We manifest our love for Mary by committing ourselves to her maternal, loving care. Let us commit ourselves to Mary regarding every aspect of our life in Christ. When we are experiencing joy, let us go to Mary. Let us share our happiness with her. Let us ask for her assistance so that we may use these times of joy according to God's designs. On the other hand, when we feel burdened with anxiety and worry, when fear makes us feel so weak and helpless, when failure and discouragement seem almost to crush us—at these times let us also look to Mary. Let us ask her to comfort us, to strengthen us. Let us further seek out Mary when we are aglow with enthusiasm, when we feel so completely permeated with dreams and desires to do great things for Christ and the world. Let us ask our mother to help us to channel this enthusiasm in a way which best serves the interests of Christ's kingdom.

Let us always thank Jesus for giving Mary to us as our mother. Let us always strive to be children who fulfill her hopes for us—that we put on Christ more and more. Let us always rejoice in the knowledge that Mary is mother at our side.

4

Some Thoughts About the Church

We are called to live our Christian existence within the Church. This is not always easy. Life within the Church is a life of death-resurrection. It can be no other way, since this pattern of death-resurrection is that of Jesus Himself.

One of the sufferings afflicting those in today's Church is the polarization between liberals and conservatives. While there will always be a certain tension between these basic groups in the Church, there is no reason why there should be an unhealthy confrontation between the two.

Both groups contribute to the life of the Church. The liberals provide an ongoing thrust for change in the Church, for adaptation of the Gospel message according to the signs of the times. The conservatives, on the other hand, caution against change for change's sake, as they give emphasis to the timeless essentials which must be present in each and every age of the Church's existence.

Yes, we hear much about liberals and conservatives in the Church. There is, however, another group which we must not overlook. This element might be called the centrists. Centrists, standing midway between the positions of the liberals and conservatives, serve as a type of mediator between the two. Without this centrist group, there would tend to be a lack of cooperation between liberals and conservatives. Centrists, among their other contributions, aid in implementing the good which both liberals and conservatives have to offer. At the same time, the centrists are in a credible position to point out the undesirable tenets of both groups.

Liberals, centrists, and conservatives—all belong to the Church which is the body of Christ. St. Paul tells us:

> *Now you are Christ's body, and individually parts of it. Some people God has designated in the church to be, first, apostles; second, prophets; third, teachers; then, mighty deeds; then, gifts of healing, assistance, administration, and varieties of tongues. Are all apostles? Are all prophets? Are all teachers? Do all work mighty deeds? Do all have gifts of healing? Do all speak in tongues? Do all interpret?* (*Cor.* 12:27-30).

The Church as body of Christ, and under the guidance of Christ, relives the mysteries of Christ. The Church obviously possesses a tremendous privilege, but also great responsibility. To continue the mission of Christ upon earth is the Church's glorious task, one given to Her by Christ Himself.

As Paul indicates above, each member of the Church has his or her particular role to fulfill in helping the Church carry out Her mission. I cannot fulfill your role, you cannot accomplish my task. We labor together, encouraging each other, laughing together, weeping together. We rejoice as our individual gifts contribute to the life of the Church. We rejoice as this Church nourishes these same gifts and gives them opportunity for expression. As we labor together, we strive to put aside the temptation of jealousy. We try to make the good of the Church our concern. We strive to promote Her works together. Who gets the credit? Really, this does not matter:

> *What is Apollos, after all, and what is Paul? Ministers through whom you became believers, just as the Lord assigned each one. I planted, Apollos watered, but God caused the growth. Therefore, neither the one who plants nor the one who waters is anything, but only God, who causes the growth. The one who plants and the one who waters are equal, and each will receive wages in proportion to his labor. For we are God's co-workers; you are God's field, God's building.* (*1 Cor.* 3:5-9).

Liberals, centrists, conservatives—we are all members of the same Church, the same body of Christ. If we cannot always agree with one another, we can always love one another. We must strive to make this love always present, always growing, always ready to overcome all difficulties for the sake of Him who has loved us first, and has laid down His life for us.

5

Eucharist—Mass

The Eucharist (The Mass) is a multi-splendored reality. It is, for example, a narrative. In the Liturgy of the Word we listen to the greatest love story of all time. It is the story of God's lavish self-communication in love to the human family throughout the course of salvation history. This story includes certain central figures, such as Moses, David, Jeremiah, Isaiah, Mary, Joseph, the Apostles, and, of course, Jesus Himself. The entire Liturgy of the Word focuses upon Christ, delineating from various perspectives this most important figure of all human history.

There are other dimensions to the Mass. The Eucharist is a memorial, as it calls to mind the life, death, and resurrection of the Lord. The Eucharist is likewise a sacrifice, an offering. This particular aspect includes all the other dimensions, and gathers them together in a wondrous unity. The Eucharist, then, is the sacramental renewal, the sign-renewal of Jesus' earthly offering. This sign-renewal contains what it signifies. Very importantly, to Jesus' offering of Himself to the Father, we add the offering of ourselves. The closing of the Eucharistic offering highlights another dimension of the Mass—the fact that it is a meal. The Eucharist as meal is rich in symbolism. Here is Jesus' self-giving love to us. Here is symbolized our commitment to Jesus, as we are intimately united to Him in the reception of the Eucharist. Here is signified our union with one another as we receive the one Christ, the sign and cause of unity among ourselves. Furthermore, the Eucharist is also a celebration—the joyous recall of the Christ event. As with all celebrations, the Eucharistic Liturgy, through its ritual, reminds us that this is a special occasion. These are some of the varied aspects of Jesus' great gift to us, the Eucharist.

From whatever perspective we approach the Eucharist, we see that participation in it involves personal contact. First of all, the Eucharist brings us into special union with God in Christ. In each Eucharist, God's communication occurs through Jesus, and this God-gift is supremely personal. God offers us love, tenderness, mercy, and a sensitive concern for our personal uniqueness, strengths, weaknesses, hopes, and fears. God invites us to come closer, and not to be afraid of the divine transforming touch. God wants us to allow the Divine Will to guide our existence amid all the myriad aspects of life within the human condition. Strengthened and inspired by the Eucharistic Christ, we are moved to say "yes" to God's invitation. With Jesus we feel warm and secure, encouraged to live out our "yes" with Him and through Him. Our fears fade into the background as we thus meet Jesus in the Eucharist, as we experience His loving embrace reach deep down where we really live. From past situations, we know that living out our response will have its share of pain, frustration, and hardship. Each Eucharistic meeting with Christ, however, reminds us that if we can do nothing without Jesus, with Him we can do all He wants of us.

As our union with Jesus deepens, we come to realize with increased conviction that His love for us and ours for Him can surmount all difficulties:

For I am convinced that neither death, nor life, nor angels, nor principalities, nor present things, nor future things, nor powers, nor height, nor depth, nor any other creature will be able to separate us from the love of God in Christ Jesus our Lord. (Rom. 8:38-39).

The Eucharist is a special source of union not only with God, but also with the members of the Christian community. Through the Eucharistic Christ we should become more aware of the bonds of faith and love that unite us. Through the Eucharistic Christ we derive the light and the strength to work against those forces which disrupt the love and unity of the Christian community— jealousies, pettiness, callous unconcern for the other, ruthless politics, backbiting, lack of teamwork, refusal to love because of wounded feelings. In union with the Eucharistic Christ we receive the light and the strength to develop those forces which build up community— selflessness, a desire to see others succeed, the supportive word, a willingness to give sincere praise for a job well done, a sense of compassion and empathy, a deep-rooted desire to really love others as one loves himself or herself.

The Eucharist, then, deepens our union with God and with the members of the Christian community. The Eucharist also deepens our union with non-Christians. The Eucharistic Christ enlightens us, strengthens us, inspires us to give of ourselves in order that the entire human family may better achieve its destiny. The Eucharist takes quiet hold of us and makes us firmly realize that everyone really is our brother or our sister. The Eucharist allows us not only to realize this awesome truth, but also gives us the desire and strength to live accordingly.

In summary, the Eucharist deepens our relationship with God, with one another, with the entire human race. The Eucharist accomplishes this in each of us—to the degree that we open ourselves to its transforming influence.

6

Faith, Hope, and Love

Faith, hope, and love are the three main Christian virtues. All the other virtues, important as they are, ultimately are at the service of faith, hope, and love. Let us look at this triad.

Today's Christian does not live in a time outstanding for its religious faith. Long ago, in the golden age of Christendom, a Christian faith-milieu was much more in evidence. Many with whom one lived and worked were co-believers. Today, a considerable part of our culture is not only non-Christian, but is also rife with secularism and hostile to religious belief. However, whatever may be the problems and difficulties relative to faith in this or any age, we know that God sustains the believer. God distributes graces commensurate with the difficulties which may confront the person of faith.

Faith gives us a new vision regarding God and all reality. Out of this vision, new relationships emerge. Faith relates us to God in a new way, and to the human family and the rest of creation.

Hope allows us to desire to live the vision of faith and to trust that God will assist us in living according to what faith proposes.

The exercise of hope does not always come easily. In

timos of greater difficulty or crisis, we realize this. Yet it is precisely at these times that we have a special need for hope. Despite the suffering, we must trust, even though the darkness seems to be enshrouding us.

God can accomplish great things through us if only we cooperate. What God accomplishes through us may, to a considerable extent, be hidden from others. True greatness, however, is still there. If we are to achieve truly great things—great in the eyes of God—we must trust. We must trust that God will lead us on to Christian maturity. We must trust that God will aid us in fulfilling our mission in life. Even at those times when we are painfully aware of how weak we are, we must trust that we can accomplish the task God sets before us. Actually, at those times during which we are especially experiencing our weakness, our optimism should grow. The more we realize our weakness, the more we should throw ourselves into the arms of Christ. We then are strong and secure in His strength. As long as we do not surrender to our weakness, we can glory in our helplessness so that the strength of Christ may support us. This was the attitude of St. Paul:

> *Therefore, I am content with weaknesses, insults. . . persecutions, and constraints, for the sake of Christ; for when I am weak, then I am strong. (2 Cor. 12:10).*

There is the virtue of faith, there is the virtue of hope, and, as the queen of all virtues, there is **love**. St. Paul reminds us, *So faith, hope, love remain, these three; but the greatest of these is love. (Cor. 13:13).*

We live successfully to the degree that we **love**. Jesus has told us this. Jesus has summarized His religion in terms of love. The Incarnation, indeed, is a work of love. In the Gospel of John we read,

> *For God so loved the world that he gave his only Son, so that everyone who believes in him might not perish but might have eternal life.* (*Jn.* 3:16).

These words remind us that our insight into the Christ-event deepens as we consider it in the light of love. Thus, we should think primarily in terms of love. Christ aids us in this endeavor by showing us His heart as symbol of God's overwhelming love for us. The heart of Christ also calls us to respond—by living our lives out of love for God and neighbor.

It is one thing to recognize the primacy of love. It is another thing to live it. Merely knowing that Christianity is summarized in terms of love is not enough. We must allow this truth to penetrate into our inner depths and to influence the way we think and act. We must consistently live according to love. We must not fall into the error which says that knowledge is virtue—that to know the good is necessarily to act accordingly. We know from painful experience that this is not true, that our activity can proceed in a direction opposite to what we know is right. We can think love, and yet act selfishly. We can know that we achieve real happiness only when we love properly, and yet we can choose to try to find happiness in other ways. We can know that our Christian personalities develop and expand through love of God and neighbor, yet at times we foolishly choose a process of self-enclosement—which is what actually occurs when we refuse to love.

Although we have sometimes failed to love as we should, we are not hopelessly depressed by this fact. We also know that many times we have cooperated with God, and we have loved. We know that in certain instances we have even surprised ourselves because of the height and the depth of our love.

Jesus, then, has come to teach us the primacy of love. He went to extraordinary lengths to impress us with this truth—that love is the chief element of Christianity. Spurred on by love's relentless drive, He embraced the horrors of Calvary's cross. He stretched out His arms on this cross, begging us not to miss His message of love, showing us that love is not measured, but lavish in its outpouring. We should have to plead guilty to an extreme insensitivity if the lesson He has so strikingly taught us makes little impression on the way we live. Let us live love, striving to live it with our entire beings, living it in full measure. This is what it means to be a committed Christian.

7

What Is Prudence?

Prudence is that virtue which helps us to make correct decisions—decisions in accordance with God's will.

It seems some have an erroneous idea concerning the nature of prudence. They think being prudent means being overly cautious, taking what seems to be the safer route, eliminating that which seems to involve risk.

Actually, Christian prudence at times will lead me to do the very bold and daring—if responsible discernment has led to the conclusion that this is God's will. It is interesting to note that even when prudence leads one to take the route fraught with risks, this decision is actually the safe one—for it is the one we responsibly think to be in conformity with God's will for us.

Prudence, or discretion, is particularly necessary in contemporary times. Both within the Church community and secular society we are faced with increased pluralism—many diverse ways of thinking and acting. Such a setting demands that the Christian strive to sharpen her or his sense of discretion. With increased frequency I must ask myself, "How does the Holy Spirit wish me to think and act?" regarding this or that issue. Amid the diversified opinions on this issue, which

seems to be correct? Or if there seems to be several correct possibilities, which does the Spirit intend for me?
Or is the Spirit telling me that none of the proposed
opinions and consequent ways of acting relative to this
particular issue are correct? Or, am I supposed to be
involved with this issue in any way? Does the Spirit
wish me to channel my energies in other directions?

A life of prayer should accompany the exercise of prudence. Prayer is a source of light which allows us to see
things as God desires. Prayer is also a source of strength
which allows us to act upon the insights prayer affords.
It is obvious that if we wish to be persons guided by a
holy discretion, we should also be persons of prayer.

8

Giving Others Their Due

The virtue of justice requires us to give others what is their due. We must respect the life, good name, and the property of others. We owe this to others because they have rights concerning these values. Also, we must give an honest day's work, and employers in turn have an obligation to pay a just wage. These, then, are some examples concerning the exercise of the virtue of justice.

We have a duty in justice, not only regarding individuals as such, but also regarding the broader scope of society at large. We have an obligation regarding the make-up of social structures and institutions. It is in this broader area of social justice that I believe we are less likely to fulfill our responsibilities.

Besides using the universal means of prayer, each of us should do what he or she can to make the various societal structures better serve the needs of all members of the human family.

There are numerous social problems facing our country and the world at large. These problems must be confronted through individual and collective effort in every way possible. Not all of us are called to be leaders in the fight for social justice, but each of us has a certain responsibility. Let us not say the social problems seem beyond solution, and, therefore, it does not much matter what we do or fail to do. This may be a handy excuse, but it does not serve the truth of the matter. Let us rather strive always to remember the teaching of the Christopher Movement: "It is better to light one candle than to curse the darkness."

In any case, there are two things we all can do, and need to do, in this area. First, we can show our involvement by example—by the life we lead, by our system of values that we show to others. Secondly, we can contribute through prayer. Prayer can change the world.

9

Coping With the Difficult

We have a tendency to try to avoid that which is hard, difficult, arduous. We must consistently strive to control this penchant; otherwise, we wallow in spiritual mediocrity.

The need for a Christian virtue which enables us successfully to encounter the difficult is obvious. Traditionally, this virtue has been called fortitude. We can also refer to it as strength of heart, or courage.

There is a long list of difficulties which are very indigenous to our human condition. Coping with failure, rejection, loneliness, and anxiety—these are all common experiences. To cope with the monotonous element of daily life without allowing it to extinguish the enthusiasm we should have in Christ's service is another challenge we must meet on a rather consistent basis. Fidelity to work and duty, even when it seems to go unnoticed and unappreciated—surely we have had to cope with this difficulty more than once.

The above are a few examples of facing the difficult which a Christian of any age could experience. Today, as we are all aware, we live in an age which has its own particular difficulties regarding both the life of the

Church and human society at large. To live in a Church which is experiencing a more than ordinary degree of change is a difficult task, no matter how optimistic we may be about the outcome. Not to shy away from our part in the renewal process, to maintain a sense of balance amid a certain amount of confusion which has accompanied change and renewal, to try to remain open and united in love with those who think and act differently than we do in today's Church—all this requires an uncommon degree of courageous dedication.

We must also consider the fact that today's Church is situated in a fast-paced and rapidly changing world, with all the problems and difficulties emanating from such an atmosphere. The crucial and difficult issues facing the human family today are staggering, and the Christian must bear her or his part of the burden. Here again the demand for courage in the face of the difficult is endless.

In conclusion, we can make the following statement: the difficulties accompanying one's presence in today's Church and the world at large, highlight the importance of the virtue of courage for successful living. Fortitude is a grace available to us from God. We all need to invoke the Holy Spirit for this gift.

10

Moderating the Pleasurable

The virtue of temperance gives us the capacity to moderate and control our tendency toward sense pleasure. It allows us to use the pleasurable according to God's will. In giving us the capacity to engage in sense pleasure properly, temperance actually increases our ability to enjoy. The temperate person can enjoy a meal more than the glutton. He or she uses the sense of taste as a human should, and, accordingly, experiences the enjoyment God has attached to the proper use of things. This satisfaction is greater than that morbid kind emanating from the wrongful use of God's creation.

We who live in affluent societies must be aware that our cultures are especially prone to excess in the matter of pleasure. If we ourselves do not avoid this excess, we not only hurt ourselves, but in various ways, we also lessen our capacity for service to others.

The virtue of temperance, then, has multiple benefits. Two of these are our greater enjoyment of the pleasurable, and the fact that temperance helps make us more fit for the greater service of God and neighbor. Self-discipline is a maturing process for all of us. It heightens our sense of responsibility while actually increasing our sense of satisfaction. The notion that all pleasure knows no bounds eventually leads to the loss of pleasure completely.

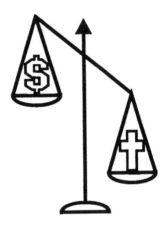

11

Humility

In our current age, we do not read or hear much concerning the virtue of humility. The spiritual masters, however, have always emphasized its importance.

Humility is realizing we are the creatures, not the Creator, and acting upon this awareness. Humility enables us to comprehend that all our gifts are from God, that without God we are nothing.

Some mistakenly think that humility means one must have a low estimate of oneself, that a person should minimize her or his gifts. This is not true. In fact, humility bids us to look at our gifts—but, very importantly, to realize the source of these gifts, God Himself. If we do not properly recognize our gifts, we will not give due thanks to God, nor sufficiently recognize our responsibility to develop these talents for God and others. Even the proper recognition that one is greatly gifted is according to the norms of humility. Mary, the mother of Jesus and our mother, is an outstanding example of this. She recognized the greatness with which God had adorned her, and, in her humility, she gave thanks to God and lived in perfect conformity to God's will.

Humility also leads us to look at what is wrong with

our existence. Humility prompts us to admit how we have failed to live as creatures of God should. Looking at our failings honestly, we determine with God's help to labor against these in order that we might be less encumbered in developing our gifts.

Not to live according to humility is to walk in nontruth, in error. Walking in error, one feels ajar, out of kilter, uneasy, lacking in desired security, fearful and anxious without fully realizing why. Failure to live according to the truth about oneself produces an unstable existence.

On the other hand, humility provides a person with a truthful perspective concerning himself or herself. Through humility a person recognizes both one's good points and bad points, and the sources of both. Being truthful about oneself, and living according to this truth, a person lives a stabilized existence, a peaceful existence.

12

On Being Thankful

On the occasion of curing a number of lepers, Jesus said:

> *Ten were cleansed, were they not? Where are the other nine? Has none but this foreigner returned to give thanks to God?* (*Lk.* 17:17-18).

This Gospel passage is a reminder to all of us that giving thanks to our Creator is an ongoing responsibility.

Father, Son, and Holy Spirit have given themselves to us in love—for this we need to be thankful. For Mary and the Church and the Eucharist—for these gifts we should also give thanks.

For life itself, for the opportunity to love and be loved, for the opportunity to accomplish the ordinary, as well as the extraordinary—for this we need to be thankful.

For the precious gift of sight which allows us to marvel at the beauties of nature and to read the printed word, for the gift of hearing which enables us to enjoy the majestic symphonic performance as well as the gleeful laughter of children at play, for the soundness of limb, for general good health which accompanies us most of our days—for all this we owe thanks to God.

For the wonderful people in our lives—for these, too,

we need to be thankful. Some of them have been extremely instrumental in helping us to be and to become. Indeed, without them perhaps we might never have grown as we have regarding certain aspects of our Christian personalities.

The pain and the joy—these permeate our lives. For coping properly with the pain, for using it as a means of growth rather than as reason for becoming bitterly self-pitied—for this grace we should give thanks to God. For the proper use of the joy in our lives, for allowing it to bring us closer to the Lord rather than permitting it to be a distraction which makes us forgetful of God— for this, too, we need to give thanks.

We should, then, endeavor consistently to be aware of the manifold and precious gifts God abundantly bestows upon us. We should resolve to maintain and develop that spirit of thanksgiving which will prevent Jesus from including us among the ungrateful: *Where are the other nine?* (*Lk.* 17:17).

13

The Need for Patience

We hear relatively little concerning the virtue of patience. Its consistent need regarding Christian living, however, is evident upon a moment's reflection. Unless a person is fundamentally patient, there is lacking that peace and acceptance which are so conducive to a reasonably happy and joyful life.

We have to be patient with others. The failings of others, their personality flaws, or just the simple fact that they possess personalities not attuned to our liking—these are some of the factors which call our patience into play. Our patience is especially tested when we suffer injustice because of the failings of others. One of the thoughts a sense of patience readily suggests in such situations is that this is an inevitable part of life, and that our own failings are also causative factors in the sufferings of others.

We must not only be patient regarding others; we must also be especially patient with ourselves. At times we can prudently avoid an encounter with certain people, and, thus, avoid patience-shattering possibilities. Regarding ourselves, however, there is no escape. Patience with the self—this is a constant and courage-demanding challenge.

Patience is required of ourselves in the never-ending cycle of customary daily duties. The sameness of daily ordinariness makes faithful performance more difficult. Patience is required to fight off feelings of boredom and lethargy arising out of the seemingly uneventful pattern which shapes our days with only minimal variation.

There are those rarer times in life which demand an unusual degree of patience. There may be a particularly grave problem crying for a solution, but the appropriate answer still eludes us—and we must patiently wait. There can also be situations which place us at a fork along the road of life's journey. The route we choose is tremendously important, yet the signs indicating God's will are not yet sufficiently clear—and we must patiently wait. At other times intense suffering piercingly enters our lives, the severity of which makes us experience each day as almost endless. We take appropriate means to try to terminate or at least alleviate the suffering, yet its end is nowhere in sight—and we must patiently wait.

The virtue of patience, therefore, should be our constant companion. Indeed, if we recognize the ongoing need for patience, we have assimilated an attitude required for a correct encounter with a variety of human experiences. Again, it is a gift—one we need to pray for.

14

Prayer

Prayer is a special dialogue in our relationship with God. In prayer we become especially aware of God's loving presence and respond with our own pledge of love. Prayer deepens our desire for God, unites us more intimately with God, and increases our determination to carry out God's will.

The best way for you to pray is that method which at any particular time seems best able to put you in contact with God. For one person this may be meditative reading—for example, prayerful reflection on a selected Scripture passage. As many passages may be prayed over as seems fruitful for a particular prayer period. For another, the best method here and now may well be a simple discussion with God concerning the happenings of one's life. Another person may choose reflection on the words of a favorite prayer. Prayer over a scene of Christ's life is another popular method. All the above are some of the common methods used in making meditative prayer. To have a deepened sense of God being present to me and I to God, and to realize that this occurs in an atmosphere of love—this is the important thing. The prayer method you use should best serve this particular purpose.

As just stated, love should permeate prayer. Christianity is a religion of love. Prayer, a particular exercise of the Christian life, should, then, also center itself in love. To realize anew how much God loves us, and to respond with a love of our own, this is the heart of prayer.

The entire Christian life, including prayer, is mediated by Christ. The Father speaks to us through Jesus:

> *In times past, God spoke in partial and various ways to our ancestors through the prophets; in these last days, he spoke to us through a son, whom he made heir of all things and through whom he created the universe. (Heb. 1:1-2).*

Christian prayer, then, is emphatically Christocentric. No matter what prayer method I use, no matter to what stage prayer develops, Christ is at the center of prayer.

If prayer is characterized by love and its Christocentrism, it is likewise marked with a spirit of openness. We must be open to what God desires to tell us, to what God asks of us. The Old Testament figure, Samuel, is a good example of this openness:

> *When Samuel went to sleep in his place, the LORD came and revealed his presence, calling out as before, 'Samuel, Samuel!' Samuel answered, 'Speak, for your servant is listening.' (1 Sam. 3:9:10).*

This attitude of openness to God in prayer is of extreme importance. This is not to say that it is always easy to make this attitude our own. There is something in us that wants to retain control of our lives, that wants us to be in charge of how our lives develop. I am not speaking of that proper and prudent sense of direction that is to be with us in the planning and execution of daily duties. I speak of that desire to control things which hinders abandonment to God. We can want to 'draw up our own agenda for living without proper reliance on the Lord. To let go, to allow God increasingly to direct our lives, takes a spiritual maturity which requires its own suffering—the pain involved in dying to that self which wants to usurp God's role in the guidance of our existence. To bear with the suffering is to achieve that joy which those alone experience who know the happiness and security resulting from casting oneself into the loving arms of our heavenly Father.

As prayer develops, it usually becomes more simplified. Beginners in the life of prayer often experience numerous ideas and images regarding God and the things of God together with varied acts of the will. As prayer develops, there usually occurs a simplification process which is threefold. First, acts of the intellect become fewer, even to the extent that one idea clearly predominates, such as "God's will be done," "Jesus is with me," or simply the realization of God's presence. The acts of the will also become fewer, and that of love more and more emerges and, in summary fashion, contains all other movements of the will. Finally, prayer's simplification process reaches out and touches everything in the person's life. She or he sees life harmoniously unified in Christ, and this simplified vision gives a sense of concentrated purpose and strength to the person's existence which was previously not present.

Prayer and its growth process are not void of all difficulties. The path of prayer, as with all spiritual life in general, is not always a smooth one. Sometimes we encounter lesser sufferings along the way; sometimes the pain is more severe. It is once again a question of death and resurrection, of pain leading to joy.

One of the common difficulties encountered in prayer is that of coping with distractions. It is only in higher mystical prayer, during which God takes special hold of the faculties, that distractions are completely absent. In the more ordinary stages of prayer, we will always have to cope with them. The challenge, then, is not to rid ourselves completely of all distractions, but to strive to bypass them when they do occur. Essential concentration on God and the things of God is still possible although distractions come and go.

Dryness in prayer is another common suffering. Often God bestows sweet consolations upon one beginning the life of prayer in order to help the person in prayer's initial stages. Often, as prayer progresses, the periods of emotionally-felt consolation become less frequent. A dryness of the emotions is noticeably present. The person, grounded in the practice of prayer, is now strong enough to continue in it even though times of consolation may be less frequent. One is learning to seek God, rather than just God's gifts of consolation. In seeking God, the person will also receive divine consolations as God chooses to give them.

As prayer becomes more simplified, at times we can be tempted to think that not much is happening. All the myriad ideas and varied movements of the will common to the beginner now significantly decrease in number. This decrease can lead us to think that prayer is less fruitful. Actually, the opposite is true. Our prayer is becoming more unified, and is penetrating more into our inner being. Consequently we must bear with this difficulty of seemingly not accomplishing much during prayer. In due time, the richness and fruitfulness of this deepened and simplified prayer will manifest itself.

Of all the difficulties encountered during prayer,

surely the most painful is to experience God as very distant. This is such a penetrating type of suffering because it strikes at the very heart of prayer—the fact that prayer is a special dialogue with God.

There are two basic reasons for God seeming to be distant. God can actually be more distant because the person is at fault. There is something of considerable significance which the person is doing and should not be doing, or something which he or she should be doing and is not. The solution to the difficulty is obvious. Corrective action should be taken. If, however, upon examination the person honestly cannot discover any such significant commission or omission, he or she can be reasonably assured this is a trial associated with prayer's growth process. Passing through this trial successfully, the person will discover that the relative darkness has turned into light, and a closer love-union with God is now experienced.

Prayer is a great gift of God. So much is gained if we consistently pray. So much is lost if we do not. Let us always remember the words of St. Paul:

Rejoice always. Pray without ceasing. In all circumstances give thanks, for this is the will of God for you in Christ Jesus. (*Thes.* 5:16-18).

15

Contemporary Asceticism

Let us define asceticism here as the effort to reach a higher spiritual level by rigorous self-discipline and denial.

Asceticism is an important element in the pattern of death-resurrection. It is one of the more active forms of dying with Jesus, for the term asceticism implies a chosen kind of effort on the Christian's part, but, very importantly, an endeavor assisted by God's grace. There is another fundamental form of the cross which does not require this more active type of effort and we could label it as passive suffering or purification, a kind of suffering which we accept in accord with God's will, but over which we have little or no control. Here, we discuss asceticism on a different level, as defined above.

The purpose of Christian asceticism is to cooperate with the Holy Spirit in achieving the necessary discipline required for the living of the Christ-life, our life of grace. This discipline is meant to extend to all dimensions of the person. As with many aspects of the Christian life, the concept of asceticism has undergone rethinking in our day. The traditional asceticism is seen as deficient in certain respects. A contemporary asceticism, geared to meet the needs of the modern Christian, has been gradually developing.

The traditional asceticism was based to a considerable extent upon the monastic or semi-monastic type of spirituality. For many centuries this spirituality was a dominant force. It became systematized and was handed down from generation to generation. Many committed Christians who were not living a monastic or semi-monastic state of life, more or less adapted this spirituality as best they could to serve their own particular vocations. As we know, this monastic spirituality stressed withdrawal from the world. If one had to live in the world, one endured it for the proper reasons, but hardly desired such a situation in itself. Many precautions were given on how to escape basically unscathed from the engagement. Monasticism's attitude toward secular involvement was to a considerable extent negative. Its asceticism was oriented toward non-involvement rather than toward proper engagement. This traditional asceticism was basically directed toward achieving a particular kind of contemplative union with God. Its direct objective was not primarily aimed at the proper building of the secular city, although it did have its own proportionate concern in this regard.

We should not be overly critical of this traditional asceticism with its stress on withdrawal, silence, and the like. It originated and developed to serve the purpose of monasticism, and in view of this goal we can say it was basically well-conceived. This spirituality certainly has produced its share of great saints. Its shortcomings arose because it came to be accepted by many as the universal asceticism—the one for committed Christians of all vocations.

As stated above, a contemporary asceticism is being developed to more realistically meet the needs of the vast majority of today's Christians. The new asceticism is meant to serve the Christian in her or his secular involvement. It is meant to help the Christian find God in the market place as well as in times of formal prayer and solitude. Its general principles can serve the needs of all committed Chritians living in the secular world, whatever their vocations may be. The traditional monastic type asceticism is still available for those living within that monastic tradition, and it has also been experiencing its own renewal.

The new asceticism, if it is to be authentic, has to meet the varied needs of the Christian in the exercise of the Christ-life. This Christ-life is a relational life. Let us now discuss three of the relationships which flow from this Christic existence—relationships with the material world, with one's neighbor, and, most importantly, with God.

The new asceticism assumes a very positive attitude toward material creation. Yet, as must the asceticism of any age, contemporary asceticism has to be concerned with the Christian's proper control relative to the material world. We have a tendency to misuse the world's material things. At times we use things in excess. At other times we use things we should not be using. These abuses are present in any age and culture, but they are apt to be multiplied among people living in affluent cultures. The new asceticism, while accepting an appreciation of material things, must also be concerned with instructing us to achieve proper control relative to the material. There are two facets of this control. One allows us to relate to the material world properly, while actually using it. The other facet directs us at times to non-use, either to learn better how to use God's material gifts, or because there is an indication that the particular use of something material is simply not according to the Spirit's designs here and now.

Turning our attention to relationship with our neighbor, let us say a few words concerning new asceticism and social concern. There is the constant temptation to settle down in the niche of one's relatively comfortable existence and act as if there were not extremely pressing social problems and issues. A Christian could even do this under pretense that he or she needs peace, a freedom from anxiety, in order to find God. The person could rationalize that to become mixed up with the murky and seething waters of social issues destroys this peace of spirit.

The asceticism of social concern points in another direction. First of all, it gives us the courage to look at the unpleasant, sometimes hideous aspects of the social structure. The asceticism of social concern bids us to reflect sufficiently about the actual situation—long enough and consistently enough so that we no longer block out that about which we should be aware. The asceticism of social concern makes us look at racism, at poverty, at the vastly destructive drug traffic, at the free reign of pornography, at political corruption—at whatever is eating away at authentic social structures, at whatever helps prevent the establishment of a more just social order.

The asceticism of social concern makes us seriously reflect on all this. Obviously, it must do more. It must also generate the verve to act upon this realization that there is much to be done. Asceticism must prompt us to embrace the pain involved in bettering the social structure, whether that pain be, for instance, enduring the anguish attendant with actual inner-city involvement, or the frustration entailed in painfully slow court procedures aimed at achieving social justice. Whatever our state of life, whatever our work or profession, whatever our immediate environment may be, the asceticism of social concern will prompt us *to do something*. This doing can range from the most intense concrete involvement of the social activist to the prayer and sacrifice of the cloistered contemplative. All of us must take Christ seriously. May He be able to say to us:

> *For I was hungry and you gave me food, I was thirsty and you gave me drink, a stranger and you welcomed me, naked and you clothed me, ill and you cared for me, in prison and you visited me.* (*Mt.* 25:35-36).

Contemporary asceticism looks not only at our responsibility toward society at large, but also at our dealings with those relatively few individuals whom we contact in a more direct and consistent fashion. There is, for example, an asceticism required for giving time and attention to the individual. This is not always easy. We live in a vastly advanced technological culture in which the individual can easily be pushed into the background where she or he tends to be treated as a faceless number rather than as an unique individual with a priceless dignity. Influenced by this ugly dimension of our culture, we can rationalize that we are too busy to give any considerable time to this or that individual. Asceticism, however, bids us to develop the patience, the loving attention, the selflessness involved in making ourselves available to individuals, particularly in those instances when the individual is not especially attractive to us.

Even when the individual is appealing to us—as, for example, in friendship or marriage—there is still an ascetical effort demanded. These close relationships are meant to be meaningful and beautiful occasions for the exercise of the deepest love. If this love is to grow and flourish, if it is not to wither, and perhaps die, there is a dying which must take place within us—it is ultimately a dying to the non-authentic self, to that self which is an obstacle to the relationship. It is a dying to that which refuses to give oneself in love so that the other may be aided in becoming more what he or she is destined to be. If these relationships are to endure properly, there must be at least a basic attitude of such selflessness. We are not speaking here of those relationships which are dissolved for legitimate reasons, for instance, a friendship which is judged by one or both parties to be no longer authentically viable.

Let us consider a few ideas concerning this new asceticism and the Christian's relationship with God. We have already said much in this regard. In discussing asceticism's role in helping the Christian relate properly to material things and to one's neighbor, we have also been implicitly speaking about one's finding God through such relationships. This is precisely one of the main thrusts of contemporary asceticism—to enable the Christian to find God in and through a proper engagement with the world.

To find God in this manner demands discipline. We have to make the effort to be open to the Spirit's guidance during our activity. We have to take the means whereby the vision of faith is vitally operative in our engagement in the market place. Following the lead of faith, we must allow Christian love to shape and inform our secular activity. If we fail to make this effort, lesser motives take over. We work and are busy, we mix in the society about us, simply because we happen to find it all so interesting, and the overriding influence of the Spirit guiding our activity fades to the background.

If we are to achieve proper openness to the Holy Spirit during our secular involvement, it seems a certain amount of formal prayer and disengagement must be structured into our lives. In this regard, the new asceticism can borrow from the traditional asceticism. Figuratively speaking, the Christian must at times go to the solitude of the desert to meet God in a more direct fashion. The Christian must seek the solitude of one's room, a church, a walk in the fields or along the lake's shore. The Christian needs these periods of disengagement in order to pray, reflect, reorient oneself so that engagement with the world may be truly a Christic one, one guided by the Spirit.

In conclusion, we can say that a new asceticism has been developing to meet the needs of today's Christian. If the current asceticism is a new one, it is not a totally different one. It is not completely differentiated from the traditional asceticism. But if it is to be really effective, today's asceticism will necessarily have to incorporate into its structure some of the practices of the more traditional one. We have just given one indication of this in our discussion of the need for a certain degree of disengagement. By having proper regard for certain teachings of traditional asceticism, the newer form can temper what could be an excessive optimism regarding our engagement with the world.

If the traditional asceticism was prone to an excessive fear of the world, the new asceticism is prone to fail to effectively point out that there are precautionary measures to be taken to ensure a proper engagement with the world. If the new asceticism can judiciously blend certain aspects of the older form with its own particular thrusts and broadened vision, then it certainly will be a more effective and realistic asceticism for the vast majority of today's Christians.

16

Self-Identity

To achieve an on-going sense of who we are in Christ is a particular way of stating the goal of the spiritual life. To become increasingly aware of who we really are, and then to live according to this awareness, is actually to live the spiritual life.

If spirituality is interested in the concept of self-identity, so also is the science of psychology. Psychologists have systems of therapy which they utilize in helping the client achieve a more stable existence. Most, if not all of these therapies involve the process of the client gradually revealing the self to the therapist. Through this process of self-revelation, the client arrives at a greater self-knowledge. He or she begins to see the reasons for the emotional and mental distress being experienced, and may gradually realize the necessary steps which are to be taken to achieve a more balanced personal existence.

We should not limit the idea of self-revelation to a client-therapist situation. Indeed, we can grow in self-knowledge—obtain a firmer grasp on our self-identity—from our general interaction with others. For example, I come to realize that I react one way with certain types of people, and another way with other people. Also, one person remarks that I have this particular characteristic 'of which I was hardly aware. Then another person makes the same observation, and I come to realize that this trait is, indeed, a dominant characteristic of my personality. If we grow in self-knowledge through a varied interaction with persons, what are we to say concerning our relationship with God? God knows us better than do all human persons taken together. Direct contact with God, then, is the chief source of growth in self-identity.

God increasingly reveals to me my Christic self. An aspect of this Christic self is my personal uniqueness. God tells me, this unique individual, that I have a special mission to accomplish.

Let us not fret, then, because we do not possess this or that particular gift, that we cannot do what this or that person so admirably accomplishes. We have the gifts God wants us to have, and we have a mission no one else can achieve.

To realize the above truths is to have a firm grasp on one's self-identity. In assimilating these truths we achieve a sense of worth, satisfaction, and purpose which admirably breeds the correct kind of self-confidence. To achieve this sense of self-identity is to eliminate that unhealthy restlessness which otherwise plagues our existence. To know who we really are is a precious gift of God.

17

Intellect, Will, Emotions

The proper balance of our intellects, wills, and emotions is most important. Overemphasis, or neglect, regarding any of these three dimensions creates hindrances to Christian living.

We can overemphasize the intellectual aspect of human nature. One example of this goes back to the time of Socrates. This famous Greek philosopher taught that to know the good is to achieve it. How many times human nature has proved him wrong! Another fallacy concerning the intellectual dimension is to think that the more we reason about an issue or problem, the better we can handle it. This approach fails to realize that not by intellect alone do we live and cope.

If our intellectual faculty can be overemphasized, it can also receive too little attention. Anti-intellectualism assumes many forms and exists in various degrees. To be intellectual beings is a great gift. To grow in proper knowledge concerning our existence and growth is a duty, not an option.

The faculty of will can also receive improper emphasis. There is a favorite axiom in our American culture—and, no doubt, in other cultures also—which says that if a person wants something badly enough, he or she can achieve that goal. This is not always the case, and unnecessary frustration and unhappiness have entered the lives of many because they have accepted this axiom and acted upon it without proper qualification.

We must not, however, underestimate the importance of the will. To use free will properly is crucial for human existence. Ultimately, our salvation depends on the correct use of this marvelous faculty called will. With our wills cooperating with God's grace, we can accomplish wonders for Christ, the Church, and the world. Not all possess great intellectual ability; this does not mean, however, that they cannot achieve great things. Our fundamental task is to conform our wills in love to God's will. The more we do this, the greater Christians we become, and the greater our achievement for Christ.

The emotions—how often they have been misused in the course of human existence. For example, uncontrolled anger has been responsible for so many human wrongs—for murder, for other acts of unjust physical violence, for all sorts of verbal slander, calumny, and vitriolic abuse. In considering another emotion, that of fear, we see a long list of human misery resulting from its improper activity. Many things have been done which should not have occurred, and many things have been omitted which should have been accomplished, because fear reigned improperly in people's lives. We also could give examples regarding other emotions, but I think the point has been made—the improper use of the emotions has caused much human misery.

The emotions are good—they come from God's creative act. Although we must be aware of their misuse, we must not fail to recognize the importance of the emotions. To fail to give the emotions their legitimate role in human existence can cause havoc to the personality.

Psychology books are replete with descriptions of what happens when the emotions are morbidly suppressed. Buried in the subconscious, the emotions can give rise to various kinds of aberrant behavior. We must not be afraid, then, to admit that we are in part emotional beings. We must not neglect to give proper expression to the emotional dimension of one person. Properly following the guidance of the intellect and will, emotions add a certain lustre, a certain vibrancy to our activity and our life.

Intellect, will, emotions—let us always strive to give each its proper place in our Christian existence. The more we do so, the more closely we follow Christ who perfectly balanced these three aspects of His human nature. As Jesus walked this earth, He showed Himself to be perfectly intellectual, perfectly volitional, perfectly emotional. Let us ourselves strive to respect the type of being God has made us—persons of intellect, will, and emotions.

18

To Be Free

If we are to follow the lead of the Holy Spirit as we should, we must possess a distinct spiritual freedom. By this I mean we must be free enough relative to persons, places, occupations—to everything—so that we might hear the voice of the Spirit and respond as we should. To put it another way, we must always be striving to relate to all things according to God's will. To do so is already to follow the Spirit's lead; to do so is also to make ourselves more free, more sensitive to the Spirit's guidance.

Some possess enough of this freedom (with its proportionate sensitivity), to hear what the Spirit is saying; but here and now they are not free enough to do what the Spirit is asking. It may be a question of ridding oneself of a particular practice, or of initiating a certain course of action. The person, however, is not free enough to respond to the Spirit's lead.

In the way I am using the phrase "spiritual freedom," I do not mean to imply the person is not responsible when this freedom is not operative. I simply mean that because of inordinate attachments, the person does not use free will properly regarding the Holy Spirit's requests.

Sometimes the shackles of our captivity possess such strength that it is only with extraordinary effort that we break loose from them. Once free, we seem overwhelmed with a new sense of spiritual vitality. We resolve to preserve our new-found freedom at all costs.

Those who have been deprived of political or other types of freedom cherish these freedoms once gained or regained. The freedom we speak of here, the freedom to do whatever God may ask, is one which calls for the deepest rejoicing; for in possessing this freedom, we are fulfilling the purpose of our existence. Is this not reason to rejoice from the depths of our being?

19

To Dwell in Peace

The necessity of maintaining ourselves in a basic spirit of peace is a key principle of the spiritual life. If we are striving to follow Christ, if we are earnest in trying to accomplish His will, then peace is meant to be ours.

There are three basic kinds of peace. One type is more of a rare occurrence. It is that which we can feel, as it were, vibrating throughout our entire being. Enjoying this particular type of peace, we feel completely alive with a joyous serenity, one which we can almost taste.

As indicated above, however, we do not often experience this exhilarating kind of peace. Our usual state is a more subdued sense of peace, one mixed in with the ordinary difficulties, discomforts, and sufferings of everyday life. If this kind of peace is more subdued, it nevertheless is a solid one which provides a proper atmosphere for walking in the way of the Lord.

The third kind of peace is similar to the first in that it is of relatively rare occurrence. For the rest, it is strikingly different from the first that we described. The peace we now speak of is that which can and should exist even in the midst of great suffering. The suffering may be some intense interior trial, or one inflicted by an outside source—which, of course, also penetrates to our interior. Whatever the intense suffering may be, and whatever its source, we should not allow it to rob us of the fundamental peace which is meant to be ours. Although we may be very troubled in the more peripheral aspect of our spirit, we can make the effort to go deep within ourselves, to the center of our being where we more directly contact God, the source of all peace. Here we stir up the well-springs of peace within us, allowing that peace to make us stable and strong despite the great suffering we are currently experiencing.

It is in the atmosphere of peace that we can best listen to the whisperings of the Holy Spirit, that we can more assuredly be open to the Spirit's touches. The more we open ourselves to the Spirit, in turn, the more we will experience peace.

Whichever kind of peace is ours at any particular juncture of our spiritual life, let us treasure it, let us pray for its increase, let us rejoice in it from the depths of our being.

Peace

20

Spiritual Guidance

Spiritual guidance is an aspect of the communal dimension of Christianity. We go to God with the help of others, and we in turn aid others in various ways along the spiritual journey. A spiritual guide is, then, one who helps us achieve Christian maturity.

The guide in spiritual matters is not out front, as it were, directing us according to some pre-conceived plan concerning how the Spirit will guide us. Of course, we must properly understand this statement. We all must follow the teaching and example of Christ. However, since we are unique individuals, the assimilation to Christ will always differ in various ways according to each one's personal uniqueness.

A key task of a spiritual guide, consequently, is to try to determine how the Spirit desires to lead this particular individual. A person seeking spiritual direction, therefore, must be willing to share his or her prayer life with the guide. This allows the guide to help the person discern the Spirit's action. A guide should not discern the Spirit's action in order that he or she may make decisions for the person being directed, but that the person himself or herself may make the proper decision in the Spirit.

And another important task of a spiritual director is to be ready to offer correction when needed. When the directee is going astray, the guide must gently but firmly point out the person's errant ways.

A common difficulty in the spiritual life, especially for beginners, is encountering discouragement. A further responsibility of the guide, then, is to help the person in coping with this obstacle. The guide must assist in developing the virtue of trust in the Lord. As trust grows, so does one's conviction that the Lord is present to us to help us deal with the various difficulties we encounter in the quest for spiritual maturity.

What about the frequency of spiritual direction? This will vary somewhat between individuals. For beginners in the spiritual journey, sessions will be more frequent than for persons more advanced. This is to be expected. There are numerous principles and practices of the spiritual life. The beginner not only must become aware of these, but must also learn how to incorporate them into his or her personal life. This is not an easy task, and the help of a spiritual director or guide is most advantageous. Sessions with a director will also be more frequent at critical points along the spiritual pilgrimage—when severe trials enter a person's life, or when one must make crucial decisions.

A good spiritual director should possess requisite knowledge concerning spiritual matters. Different degrees of knowledge are necessary depending upon the types of persons one directs. A guide who directs persons blessed with mystical prayer should be conversant with the ways of mysticism, whereas such knowledge is not strictly necessary for the guide who works with those traveling the more ordinary paths.

In choosing a director one must determine as best as

possible whether that person seems to possess the knowledge requisite for giving competent advice.

Good spiritual guidance is a gift of God. If such guidance is not reasonably available, God will compensate. If it is available, one should not disdain it, but utilize it as one of the providential means afforded us in the quest of putting on Christ.

21

Our Weakness and Our Strength

St. Paul tells us, *I will rather boast most gladly of my weaknesses, in order that the power of Christ may dwell with me* (*2 Cor.* 12:9). This brief passage contains one of the greatest lessons of the spiritual life. As we progress along our spiritual journey, we become increasingly aware of how weak we are in ourselves, but how strong we are in Christ.

To experience our weakness involves suffering. The degree of suffering can vary, culminating in the very painful experience of the classical "dark night" of the spirit or its equivalent. St. John of the Cross has vividly described the sufferings of this classical dark night.

One of the main purposes of the dark night is to make a person keenly aware of his or her helplessness without God. This is a most necessary point that mystics must pass through if the spiritual marriage, or transforming union with God, is to occur. In this transforming union, there is a profound exchange between God and the mystic. God's self-communication to the mystic is most profound, and the mystic makes a profound gift of self to God. In this state the mystic is supremely aware of living by the life of God, and without experiencing one's helplessness without God, this lived awareness does not occur.

If not all on the spiritual journey experience the classic dark night, all must undergo a proportionate purification which includes increased awareness of personal weakness. In this process one more and more abandons the self to Christ and increasingly lives by His life, by His strength. St. Paul says,

> *...I live, no longer I, but Christ lives in me; insofar as I now live in the flesh, I live by faith in the Son of God who has loved me and given himself up for me.* (*Gal.* 2:20).

How much the Christian process of growth differs from that which many psychologists propose for personality fulfillment, a process which depends, say these psychologists, solely on the efforts of one's own will power. The Christian, omitting the errors of psychology, can, of course, utilize what is helpful from psychological teaching and properly integrate it into the Christian theology of personality growth. This theology teaches that God's grace is absolutely necessary. Though our efforts are indeed indispensable along the spiritual journey, the human effort can only be correctly understood as a response to God's loving initiative. This very response is God-assisted, made possible by God's love-given grace.

Our sense of weakness is not a paralyzing one. It does not hinder our performance of duty. On occasion, athletes and other performers may, for various reasons, feel very inadequate regarding the exercise of their particular skill. This sense of inadequacy, in turn, can detract from performance. In the spiritual life, however, our sense of weakness does not impair our capacity to function as

Christians. On the contrary. If, sensing our helplessness, we increasingly abandon ourselves to Christ, we act with greater spiritual vitality. We do this with a basic peace of which the world knows not.

Indeed, to those who are unspiritual, the concept of striving to grow through the sense of our weakness is complete folly, utter craziness. To those who have received the gift of the Holy Spirit, however, being properly aware of one's weakness is strength and peace and consolation.

22

Creativity

To be creative is one of the great joys of being human. We should resolve to more consistently stir up the spark of creativity which each of us has in various degrees. Most of us cannot be magnificently creative as was Michelangelo in sculpting his Pieta, which still attracts marvelled attention of thousands as it sits majestically in Rome's St. Peter's Basilica. Most cannot stir the emotions with the musical genius of a Beethoven, or breathtakingly portray the inner depths of a person as does a Rembrandt portrait. We cannot move the minds and hearts of countless people as do the magnificent literary pieces of William Shakespeare.

These are all obvious examples of the human capacity for creativity. There are, however, many other less brilliant possibilities. Being less brilliant does not mean they are not greatly worthwhile.

There are numerous ways we all can be creative. One person arranges a yard in very ordinary fashion. A more creative individual does so in a manner which presents flowers, shrubs, and trees in a most attractive setting. One teacher presents material in a clear, but unimaginative way. Another, using diverse and creative methods, stirs up the students' interest in a manner which makes learning a joy. One director stages a play in competent but rather uninspiring fashion. Another, directing the very same play more creatively, draws out the talent of the actors to a maximum degree, and the applause of the audience to thunderous proportions. One person is not particularly creative in his or her personal relationships; another manages to add ongoing vitality with ingenious touches of newness, of creativity.

We do not all have the same talents. Nor will we find satisfaction in just trying to imitate the special talents of others. We all need to discover what gifts the Lord has given to us—each of us.

Whatever we do, then, let us strive to bring a sense of creativity to the task or activity. God has given us a creative capacity. Let us resolve to use it. In doing so, we will be more alive, and we will also help those we contact to grow in the appreciation of the vitality of human existence.

23

Special Days

There are certain days which make us feel especially glad to be alive. Often—but not always—the weather is consonant with our inner feelings. If it happens to be fall, the air is crisp, quickened with October freshness. The leaves spellbind us with their rich and varied colors— their golds, and reds, and browns. The sky is autumn blue, clear blue, crowned with a golden sun. Or, if it happens to be spring, a deep and fresh greenness seems to cover everything, breathing forth new signs of hope for the world. A gentle breeze mixes with the sun's warmth in a perfect mixture which makes us eagerly seek the out-of-doors.

Inside—inside ourselves—things are also especially beautiful on these very special days. We feel aglow with the beauty of life. Life has a mysterious freshness on these days, making us especially aware of its grandeur, its tenderness, its expansiveness, its capacity to call us forth to greatness. On such days the splendid drama of life deeply attracts us, lays hold of us in those inner depths where we are most alive, where we are most ourselves.

We need these days on which we feel deeply alive. If such days did not periodically refresh us with their pleasant arrival, then boredom and the monotonous aspect of daily living, the drudgery of life, would be too much for us. As the little child needs to be especially cheered on occasion by a surprise gift of candy or a toy, so all of us need periodic excursions into the realm of these special kinds of days. They, too, are often pleasant surprises, for usually we cannot forecast their advent with any degree of precision.

We should make the most of these special days. They are precious gifts which God lovingly offers us. Through them God enlivens the ordinariness of our lives, and gives us the desire to refurbish what may have become a rather lethargic type of existence. We can fall into a rut of wasting many of the opportunities which each day presents. Our lethargic condition can cause us to squander much of life's precious moments. We must allow the beauty of the special kind of day we have been describing to once again enliven our appreciation of the value of life. We must determine not to squander existence, but to drink in its preciousness from the depths—this preciousness which offers us countless opportunities to reach out for the good, the true, and the beautiful.

24

Anxiety, Fear, And Worry

The fear of financial insecurity, the fear of not being accepted by others, the fear of professional failure, anxiety concerning whether one is capable of handling an inevitable crisis, the spectre of academic failure, the fear of being rejected in love, worry about the illness of a loved one—these are some of the myriad anxieties, fears, and worries we encounter along the varied path of life. Life twists and turns, now stretches out straight, now descends into the valley, now ascends where the horizon can be clearly seen.

To encounter worry, fear, and anxiety during the course of life is to be expected. To allow these disturbances to conquer us and to rob us of basic peace of spirit is to react incorrectly. To face anxiety, fear, and worry with Christian courage and trust is to live by the words of Jesus:

> *Are not five sparrows sold for two small coins?*
> *Yet not one of them has escaped the notice of*
> *God. Even the hairs of your head have all been*
> *counted. Do not be afraid. You are worth more*
> *than many sparrows. (Lk. 12:6-7).*

We can cause ourselves various problems if we do not

properly handle fear, worry, and anxiety. We lose some of the joy of life. We stunt our personality growth, making ourselves less attractive to others. We threaten our emotional and physical health. We lessen our effectiveness of being witnesses to the good news, to the fact that Jesus' truth is meant to free us from enslavement, including that of morbid fear and worry.

Why then do we not take Jesus at His word? He tells us not to be unduly worried. He tells us there is really no reason to be overly anxious about anything. He loves us, the Father loves us, the Holy Spirit loves us. They love us infinitely more than we love ourselves. Their love can basically cut through the bonds of any fear, any worry, and anxiety. Yes, their love can do this—if we so permit.

25

A Sense of Priorities

Often people remark after surviving a very traumatic situation. "It makes you realize what is really important in life. It makes you see things in a different perspective."

All of us must constantly strive to maintain proper perspective, and it is not easy. If we reflect on what commands our time and attention, we realize that often we have a tendency to overemphasize the less important and to undervalue the more important.

Examples of this are numerous. At times we attach more importance to a sporting event or to the latest top-rated movie than to a pressing social issue. The status of one's wardrobe can cause more concern than the status of one's spiritual condition. Within family circles, material possessions can come to mean more than the personal relationships which the material things are meant to serve. These are only a few examples of distorted priorities.

In many ways we can come to regard the trivial as all-important, the non-essential as essential, the ephemeral as something that will last forever, the means as more important than the end, the less important as the more

73

important. In brief, our priorities can become terribly distorted, and to the extent that our priorities are in disarray, to that degree we are wasting our existence.

To achieve a proper sense of priorities, and to live according to the values inherent in these priorities, we must give time to prayerful reflection. This contemplative exercise gives us the light to see issues according to a proper hierarchy of importance. Very critically, this time of prayer also gives us the strength to live according to this light. Is there anyone who really believes he or she does not have time to pray? If there is such a person, we have a classic example of one whose priorities are wretchedly confused.

If our first priority is Jesus Christ, and saving our soul, all the rest of our priorities will fall into the proper slots in our life.

26

Shattered Dreams

To hear the words "shattered dreams" conjures up for us memories of major disappointments experienced along the ever-changing path of life. The disappointments can be those which wound the heart to its core. Disappointments of lesser proportions cause diminished pain, but still a kind which leaves its mark.

Shattered dreams come in all sorts of sizes and shapes. Some experience career disappointments even though they were privileged to enter the work of their dreams. Once professional success was achieved, however, a type of emptiness ensued and, with puzzlement, they asked themselves, "Is this all the satisfaction that comes from all my strivings? Is this all there is to professional success?"

Others experience shattered dreams because the careers they hoped for were always beyond their grasp. For this or that reason they were not able to give themselves completely to that work or occupation for which their hearts yearned. For example, one with outstanding talent as an artist can only give a bit of free time to expressing his or her genius because financial problems force the person to work full-time at another occupation. The heartbreak this occasions can only be known by one who has experienced this kind of frustration. An athlete on the verge of national stardom sustains a serious injury which necessitates abandonment of a cherished sport. These and similar examples leave one with the question: "What would it have been like?...I'll never know."

Personal relationships have yielded a plethora of shattered dreams. A person experiences crushing disappointment because he or she is rejected by a person dearly loved, a person who had been the focus of so many hopes and dreams. Another experiences pain because the hoped-for relationship with a particular person never eventualizes. In both cases tears flow copiously and the person has to strive mightily to convince oneself that life is still worth living.

The shattered dreams of parents regarding their children—this particular kind of pain makes up a considerable portion of life's sufferings. For example, a child with so much to live for is snatched away in sudden, unexpected, and tragic death. Or parents watch a child slip away from their influence and go the way of moral degradation despite the parents' best efforts to provide proper guidance. Other situations involve financial problems which prevent the desired education of exceptionally gifted children—an education the parents had so much hoped for.

There are many examples of shattered dreams. You know of other examples, ones which you have personally suffered, and others which you have seen others experience. All examples involve shattered hopes, whose remains are scattered about in the form of burnt-out ashes, the remnants of goals once eagerly sought, but which now no longer exist.

As Christians we too are subject to experiencing shattered dreams along with the rest of the human race. However, being exposed to various disappointments will not excessively disturb us if we rely on our Christian perspective. To be able to view disappointment in union with Christ is a great gift which all do not possess.

With the light afforded by this Christian perspective, we should ask ourselves whether the shattered dream was the result of seeking that which was outside of God's will. Sooner or later such a pursuit always causes a sense of emptiness, disappointment, disillusion. Disappointment can also result from the relative failure of doing that which we thought to be Spirit-inspired. The disappointment attached to such a venture, however, is permeated with a distinct sense of peace; for we realize we have done our reasonable best to follow God's lead. Our effort has failed in one sense; but in another sense, we have succeeded. We know that good has emanated from our conformity to God's will.

Individual shattered dreams do not destroy the all-pervading dream or hope of the Christian. We know that if we remain basically faithful to Christ, our dream, or hope, regarding our earthly destiny will be fulfilled. We further know that this dream or hope for a truly successful existence on this earth will open up to absolute fulfillment in eternal life. The committed Christian, then, can experience shattered *dreams,* but not a shattered *life,* for in them we can also recognize a challenge and a cross to carry. He has asked us to pick up our cross and follow Him.

27

Limitations

We are finite creatures. By this very fact we have limitations of various sorts. We must, however, distinguish between false limitations—those which need not be—and those which legitimately emanate from our finitude.

False limitations are those which, for various reasons, we wrongfully inflict upon ourselves. Let us consider some of these.

There is that limitation with which we are burdened when we waste time comparing ourselves with others. We say that if we possessed the talents of this or that person, well certainly *then* we could achieve great things. All the while, we partially waste the gifts we do possess. We miss numerous opportunities for serving God and others because we foolishly squander time and attention bemoaning the fact that we lack this or that talent.

We also needlessly limit our possibilities for achievement when we choose a type of work for which we are ill-suited. Many times necessity does not demand we choose such occupations or remain in them. It is rather our failure to use reasonable means to ascertain what occupations will best utilize our talents.

We also suffer unnecessary limitations when we fail

to generate the proper motivation which would allow for the reasonable development and implementation of our gifts. Properly motivating ourselves is something we must consistently strive for. The kind of motivation that thrusts us forward at one stage of our life and in one set of circumstances may well not be the particular motivating factor we need at other points of life's journey.

There are numerous limitations which need not be. There are also limitations which are inevitable. There are, for instance, situations which limit the use of the talents we actually do possess, and there is little or nothing we can do to change these circumstances. At other times when we do have the opportunity to exercise our talents we realize, sometimes with painful awareness, that there is only so much time and energy. We realize we must leave much undone precisely because of such restraints. There are also those situations in which, despite our own good will, we are limited in what we can accomplish because of the disinterest and even hostility of those we are trying to serve.

Let us pray for the gift to be able to distinguish between those limitations which need not exist and those which are inevitable. Let us also pray for the strength to eliminate those limitations which need not be. Finally, let us ask for the courage to endure patiently those restrictions which are beyond our power to remove.

28

Past, Present, and Future

We are past, present, and future persons. There is a certain connection between these three dimensions of our existence, but, very importantly, there is also a distinction.

We are past persons. This we cannot deny. The past, to a certain extent, shapes our present and our future. For example, the past can be a good teacher. Aware of past mistakes and successes, we can now guard against the former, and be in better position to repeat the latter.

We must also guard against the negative influence of the past. We must, for example, avoid the morbid dwelling on past mistakes and missed opportunities. Such an exercise only lessens our capacity for present accomplishment and future planning. Yes, let us learn from the past, but let us not be held its captive.

We are also future persons. This future includes the time yet remaining for us here upon earth, as well as that absolute future which is full union with God in eternal life. Looking ahead to our absolute future includes thoughts about our future days upon earth. We must plan for this future with a sense of Christian purpose and prudence. Also, we must allow ourselves to be motivated continually by goals not yet achieved, but which beckon us with an enthusiasm to achieve still more for God and neighbor.

If we are past and future persons, we are also present persons. This may be the most difficult. We can dwell too much on the past, a process which robs us of energy for present accomplishments. Disproportionate thinking about the future can also detract from the attention the present deserves.

I believe one of the persistent temptations which we must confront regarding the present is the tendency to underestimate the importance of our life here and now. For example, we can be tempted to think that our time for significant accomplishments has not yet arrived—an attitude which detracts from the attention and commitment we should give to the task at hand.

One of the greatest challenges of the spiritual life is to give ourselves as fully as possible to the present situation. Indeed, one of the best criteria for judging spiritual progress is one's ability to attach to the present the importance it deserves. Traditional spiritual literature has often discussed this critical attitude toward the here and now as the concept of the sacrament of the present moment.

Giving proper attention to the present demands a consistent expression of the various Christian virtues. For example, it requires the exercise of faith, hope, and love. Faith shows us that each day, as ordinary as it may outwardly appear, is a new and marvelous opportunity to be and to become for God and others. Love, in turn, eagerly embraces this faith-vision and propels us to loyal service within the prosaic framework of everydayness. Hope in the Lord must also accompany us each day— trust that He will aid us in coping with various difficul-

ties which, if not properly confronted, hinder our fulfillment of present obligations.

Patience is also necessary to successfully cope with
everydayness. We can be tempted to withhold proper
devotion to the present because some of its tasks involve
commitment over an extended period of time, whereas
we would prefer the quick arrival of successful results.
Let us remember that many before us initiated the works
we now enjoy in their finished stage. Those who began
these enterprises had to labor at them knowing that they
would not see the culmination of their dedicated efforts.

To properly give ourselves to the present necessitates
that we also exercise a spirit of forgiveness. Harboring
bitterness and hatred toward those who have wronged
us only robs us of the serenity and energy we need for
present accomplishments.

Humility must likewise accompany us in our dedication to the here and now. We can be tempted, however
subtly, to think the present task is not worthy of our best
effort. Humility reminds us that whatever God's will
puts before us each day does indeed demand our full
commitment.

Without further extending our discussion of the Christian virtues, it is obvious that giving proper attention to
the present challenges our spiritual capacity in a variety
of ways.

We are past, present, and future. Let us allot each of
these dimensions its proper role. Let us remember that
we can best respect the past and prepare for the future
by the proper utilization of the present. St. Paul tells us:
*Behold, now is a very acceptable time; behold, now is
the day of salvation. (2 Cor.* 6:2).

29

A Sense of Being Overwhelmed

Sometimes life can seem to overwhelm us, at times
with surprise and suddenness, at other times with clear
signs that we are now about to experience human existence as a sort of massive deluge. During these times of
seeming to be overwhelmed, we obviously feel more
than uneasy, and at times deeply anxious. We lack that
sense of being in reasonable control of things.

There are various factors contributing to our sense of
being overwhelmed. People, various circumstances,
places, happenings—all these help shape the situation.

Moreover, it is not only the unpleasant side of life
which is always the causative factor. Sometimes the joyful, the happy, the ecstatic dimension of human existence can produce the sensation of being overwhelmed.
There is the instance of great happiness coming into our
lives. In the midst of overflowing joy we begin to won-
der how long it will last—it all seems too good to be
true. We feel somehow incapable of properly handling
and assimilating such a huge portion of life's happiness.
Similarly, occasions of outstanding and astonishing success can also overwhelm us. We feel partially at a loss
on how to cope with such extraordinarily good fortune.
We feel ourselves being on unfamiliar ground. The way

to react to such success seems to elude our thinking, and life suddenly is filled with various uncertainties.

Very obviously, the darker and more somber side of life also makes us feel overwhelmed. There is the situation involving crucial decision-making. We wish the decision were not ours; but the more we engage in such unrealistic thinking, the more the anguish of the situation presses upon us. Suddenly it seems as though the whole of life hinges upon what we choose to do. The magnitude of the decision and its consequences can make us feel almost helpless. We feel so alone, so overwhelmed.

Certain individuals, those very precious persons in our lives, can bring about this experience of life-seeming-too-big-to-handle. It may be the loss through death of one deeply loved. The lost one was such a part of us, so deeply ingrained in us, that we feel that a major part of our own self has perished along with the loved one. Confronting life now seems like such a threatening proposition and there seems to be hardly any psychic energy or inclination for the struggle. At times people precious to us can create this burden, not by physically dying, but by dying in another fashion. It can be a case of alcoholism, or drug addiction, or serious moral depravity, or insanity. "How can I go on living?" we ask ourselves, and the answer comes not from our feelings, but from the fact that we actually do make it through another day.

Life also overwhelms us at those times when devastating failure so harshly visits us. The failure destroys a large portion of our life's hopes and dreams. Whatever the type of crushing failure, life, temporarily at least, seems like a burnt-out vessel, and the remaining ashes only serve to remind us bitterly of happier days.

Whatever may be the cause of our being especially aware of the awesomeness, the overwhelmingness of life—and we have mentioned only a few of the possibilities—we can best confront the situation if we deepen our realization of a most consoling truth. We engage in life's journey, so frightening at times, not alone. We have the support of those we can reach out and touch, those who are walking the path of life with us. We also have the support of the One, who, although we cannot physically touch, we can contact through our faith, hope, and love. This One is our friend, Jesus. He wants to share life with us. He wants us to realize how closely present He is to us. He wants us to draw upon His loving presence at all times, especially on those occasions when the burdens in life seem to be engulfing us.

30

Avoiding Mediocrity

Even after years of close friendship with Jesus, a Christian can decide to make a radical break and go his or her own way. In the mysterious depths of our free will, we can decide, for whatever reason, to no longer walk side by side with Jesus. This Jesus, who inspires to the greatest heights, who manifests an overwhelming mercy, who whispers His loving and tender concern—this Jesus is now rejected. Indifference replaces commitment.

On a lesser scale—and perhaps this is what happens much more often than does outright rejection of the Lord—a Christian can refuse a deep closeness with Jesus while still fundamentally maintaining the friendship. In other words, the person opts for mediocrity. Jesus keeps calling the person to a more dynamic Christian existence, but the person keeps resisting.

To choose mediocrity is to choose immaturely. The only mature choice is to strive to live out the full implications of being a follower of Jesus. In making such a choice, we experience our share of suffering. At times this suffering tests our love and our courage to the utmost. The suffering, however, is for the positive purpose of extending Christ's kingdom, and an aspect of this is our own closer union with Jesus.

If we are to avoid mediocrity, we must avoid that attitude which says, "I will go so far with you Jesus, but no farther. I want to come close to you Jesus, but not too close. If I come too close, you might ask something of me which is very difficult." We know in the depths of our hearts that this is a foolish attitude—for when has Jesus ever asked anything of us and not given us the grace to accomplish it? When has Jesus ever asked anything of us which was not intended for our greater happiness?

31

Failure

One of the most painful sufferings we experience
within the human condition is failure. The suffering is
often exacerbated because we over-identify with the situation. We have linked too much of our being with the
task, the relationship, or whatever else has prompted the
failure. We tend to think, for example, that because we
have failed in a particular work, we have failed as
human beings. However, as much as we may have
involved ourselves in the work, we are not the work
itself. This is not to say we are always blameless. We
may be considerably at fault regarding the failure. On
the other hand, we may be basically without culpability.
Whichever the case, we must strive not to over-identify
with the situation. This only increases the pain, and
needlessly so.

Besides over-identifying with failure, there are two
other sufferings connected with it. There is very obviously the pain of the failure itself—even when we succeed in keeping it within proper perspective. There is
also the pain of regrouping, of starting over, of getting
on with the rest of life. This is not easy; but the pain
involved is less than that which results from remaining
mired in the failure, allowing it to rob us of some of the

joy which is meant to be ours. There have been, are, and will be failures of various kinds and degrees in our lives. Let us accept the pain involved, learn from it, and continue the spiritual journey as wiser human beings.

32

Loneliness

Loneliness is an experience which afflicts every human being to one degree or other. No one escapes its suffering. Its pain can vary from being no more disturbing than that of other common sufferings, to a kind of affliction which penetrates to one's inner depths and makes one shed copious tears.

There are two basic kinds of loneliness: the one which need not be, and the one which is inevitable. The one which is avoidable emanates from our not relating to God and others as we should and can. The other, which exists even though we are doing our reasonable best to reach out to God and neighbor, is simply a part of the human condition. We experience an unavoidable loneliness because we are pilgrims. Until our pilgrimage ends in the attainment of eternal life, loneliness will always haunt us in various degrees. This must be, for the kind of loneliness which is inevitable results from our not yet being completely fulfilled. We attain perfect fulfillment only in eternal life. Until then we are, in part, lonely creatures.

If unnecessary loneliness results from our not relating properly to God and others, the remedy for lessening its suffering is obvious. We must strive to grow in our relationships with God and others. This is not going to completely remove loneliness, but it will lessen its pain and make it more bearable.

In coping with loneliness we experience ups and downs in the process, and even apparent contradictions. For example, in striving to deepen my relationship with a significant person—a step which basically lessens loneliness—I may still experience it on occasion because of prolonged physical separation from this person, or because of misunderstandings which temporarily seem to separate us to some extent. Regarding God, at times one can feel a particular loneliness precisely because one desires God so much; but for now, God seems hidden and difficult to contact. Some experience this suffering in a very penetrating fashion as they undergo the classical dark night of the spirit; others feel this loneliness in a less striking, but still very real, fashion.

Loneliness resulting from our efforts to relate properly to God and others is not debilitating as is that which emanates from our failure to go out to God and others as we should. This is so because the former constitutes part of the positive growth process.

The temptations which confront the human person in his or her struggle with loneliness are numerous and well known. Seeking alleviation from loneliness in alcohol and other drugs, in illegitimate sex, in excessive TV watching—these are a few of the escape routes well known to the modern world. Whatever the false escapes, they seem to be more prevalent in affluent cultures where money can buy practically any false comfort one could desire.

Here in the United States, the affluent American can easily buy all the non-authentic escapes from loneliness. These false routes beckon us so enticingly, promising a quick solution to our problem. As with anything non-authentic, however, embracing them as a cure for loneliness actually makes the problem more severe. So it is not surprising that a group of experts has concluded that loneliness is a serious problem in today's world, and nowhere does it seem to be greater than in the United States.

In coping with the problem of loneliness, we should look at the phenomenon realistically. This realistic view tells us that loneliness will always be with us to some degree. Dealing with the problem does not mean eradicating all loneliness. It means making sure that we are not causing ourselves unnecessary loneliness by failing to relate to God and others as we should. In other words, it means we should strive to love as we should. The person who is trying to love properly is not a person who escapes all loneliness. He or she is a person whose basic happiness, loneliness does not destroy.

33

Facing the Day's Task

There are times when we eagerly face each day and the tasks it holds for us. There can be numerous reasons for our enthusiasm. For example, recent successes have bred a newfound confidence, and we gladly face the new day's challenges. A very important goal soon to be achieved can also offer special motivation to embrace the day's work with added verve. Whatever may be the reasons for making us eager to face the coming day, we feel especially grateful for being alive.

At other times we can feel a type of dread at the thought of tackling the day's tasks. Sometimes the cause of this dread is evident to us. At other times, the reason is more nebulous, and our trying to analyze the situation yields unsatisfactory results. Whatever may be the cause of our lack of enthusiasm, we know we must work through the depression the dread has produced. When we do push ourselves forward to confront the day's work, we often find the sense of dread dissipates in the very doing of the work itself. The problem we originally experienced is transformed into a sense of satisfaction, and even enthusiasm, regarding the work at hand.

Amid the different moods which can color our attempts to face each day's tasks—and we have mentioncd only a few—we must be looking toward growth. We must strive to become persons who are more sensitive to the needs of others. We must be aware of the fact that there is so much evil to be overcome. We must also be very much aware that the goodness in the collective human heart outweighs the evil, and that we must help this goodness to more deeply permeate the various dimensions of life within the human condition.

Face the fact that we are all merely human beings. And as such, we all have good days and bad. From the greatest to the smallest, none have escaped, but Jesus was ready to walk through it with all of them, as He is with us.

Briefly, we must always be desirous of accomplishing our mission in life with greater love of God and neighbor. Now is the time to start, for there will come a day which has no tomorrow.

34

The Tenderness of Life

Life can be hard. Sometimes the harshness of life seems on the verge of overwhelming us. To maintain a proper balance, we need alleviation from this harsh edge of human existence. We require means whereby its effects are softened or compensated for. One such means is to allow the tenderness of life to exercise its proper role. God intends this. God has inserted the touch of tenderness within the work of his creation. We see many examples of this in the animal kingdom. A mother dog, for instance, playfully and tenderly paws her little pups.

God has also made the human heart for tenderness. The heart of Jesus offers a perfect example of this, for more than once Jesus manifested a sense of tenderness. We can picture Jesus saying,

> *Jerusalem, Jerusalem, you who kill the prophets and stone those sent to you, how many times I yearned to gather your children together, as a hen gathers her young under her wings, but you were unwilling!* (*Mt.* 23:37).

God has made us to experience touches of tenderness, and we need to open ourselves to this tenderness of life.

If we do not, can we long endure the pain and brutality of human existence? If there were not touches of tenderness, who could endure experiencing the death of loved ones, or sickness, or emotional distress, or loneliness?

The tenderness of life comes to us in many diverse forms. There is the tenderness which unites man and wife—the touch and the look and the kiss of tenderness. There is the maternal touch of tenderness—and because of it the baby feels secure, wanted, loved. There is the warm, receptive smile of a friend. The gentle, encouraging word is also a form of tenderness. Husky athletes visiting a hospital for children offer a touching scene also. Perhaps clumsily, yet very sincerely and tenderly, these hulking men will stroke a young brow or caress the hair of a disabled girl. Food delivered to the poor at Thanksgiving and Christmas are other reminders that the tender concern of the human heart still looks out for the world's disinherited. A mother, tearfully and joyfully embracing her son returned from war's battlefields, is a classic example of life in its tenderness. Two little boys, one black and one white, hugging each other in their gleeful playfulness offer a scene which can move the hearts of even those calloused with considerable prejudice.

Nature also offers us signs of tenderness. There is the delicate touch of snowflakes against the cheek or the gentle fall of a steady rain. Rolling meadows offer their soft greenness for joyful picnics as the gentle breeze lies tender against the brow made warm by the summer sun.

We can act sophomorically and tell ourselves we do not need the tenderness of life, saying that to be very much concerned with it is a sign of childishness or weakness. We can say all this—but that will not change the fact that God has delicately woven the touch of tenderness into the tapestry of human life. Tenderness is just one aspect of our human existence, and to be properly open to it will make us more human and happier than we would otherwise be.

35

Work and Workaholicism

To work hard for God and others is obviously a desirable trait. To be a workaholic, however, is to be burdened with an unhealthy personality characteristic.

What is the difference between the two? Is it the amount of time devoted to work? No, because some people who are not workaholics may spend as much time working as does the workaholic. Does the difference consist in the fact that the workaholic derives more satisfaction from his or her efforts than others do? No, because the non-workaholic may actually derive more enjoyment from work than his counterpart.

What then is the difference? The difference seems to consist in the workaholic's more or less compulsive need to work. Such a person feels uneasy and restless unless he or she is busy. Only work seems to have meaning for the person.

All of us, workaholics or not, should reflect on our attitude toward work. As important as it is, work still is just a means to an end. In the Christian perspective, it is an expression of our love for God and neighbor.

Upon reflection, we can see the consequences of this. When work, for whatever reason, is interfering with our relationships with God and others, something is obviously amiss. For example, an upward-moving professional becomes so absorbed in his work, so taken with the idea of promotion and salary increase, that he becomes extremely narrow-minded. Concern for God and others is relegated to the far recesses of consciousness where it has little effect upon the person's thoughts and activities.

Even though we claim such an extreme situation does not describe our own, we nevertheless can fall prey to lesser faults. For instance, we diminish the time we should rightfully be spending with family members and friends. Perhaps we also become so absorbed with our work that we claim we have little time for prayer. When we find ourselves in such circumstances, we must make the effort to confront ourselves with the question, "What is the purpose of my work, of my professional activity?" Surely, if we are honest, we must say that our efforts should be for God first. If we work with this proper motive, we are acting for our own benefit also, for what is done for God and others promotes our own good.

Our contemporary society places much emphasis on external success, the attainment of recognition for one's work, and the earning of more and more money—and all this in a very secularistic manner with little regard for God and neighbor. In such an atmosphere, it is not easy to maintain the Christian perspective of work. In many ways we must go counter-culture if we are to live by this Christian vision. If we do so, we will be following one who Himself was not afraid to go against certain cultural aspects of His own times. His name is **Jesus.**

36

Involvement with the World

The world belongs to Christ. Because of our love for Christ, we must be concerned with that which is His. It is the Christian's duty, therefore, to share responsibility for furthering the world's progress according to the designs of its Creator.

Our love for neighbor also prompts us to be concerned about the world. We and our neighbor do not live in a vacuum. We are affected by the type of world which surrounds us. If we say we love our neighbor—and ourselves—we must do our part in helping to make this a better world in which to live.

There are two radically different ways in which one can be involved with the world—the incorrect way and the proper way. The incorrect type of involvement has often been called secularism—secularism being that view of the world which has little or no role for God and religion. The correct manner of involvement is, of course, to follow the lead of God's will. God calls all of us to some engagement with the world. Contrary to what some think, the monk also must have a concern for the world according to his vocation. It is not a question of whether or not to be involved with life in the market place. We must rather ask, "How does God want me to be involved?"

We are involved in the world in either a more individualistic way or in a more communal manner. Both ways have their advantages.

The more individualistic way has the advantage of presenting us with a constant opportunity to help promote the world's goodness and to work against its evil aspect. This manner of involvement simply consists in our carrying our Christian principles into the market place. Whatever we do should spring forth from these principles. In this way, although we may not be attracting much notice, we are doing our share to help further develop the world's God-given goodness.

The other manner of involvement—the more communal way—brings us together in group activity. It is a situation of being united with others to promote this or that good. The advantage of group activity is twofold: it provides corporate support and encouragement, and it usually has greater impact than do mere individual efforts.

These two ways complement each other, so let us then use both. There is so much to be accomplished. Let us labor while there is still time. Jesus has left us these words:

> *We have to do the works of the one who sent me while it is day. Night is coming when no one can work. (Jn. 9:4).*

37

The Self and Others

Did you ever stop to think about how much we depend on others? Consider a simple breakfast of orange juice, toast, egg, and coffee. It is amazing to reflect on the number of people involved in enabling us to partake of this simple meal. There are the farmers who produced the ingredients, the people who made the farmers' equipment, the various food processors who receive the farmer's goods, the truck drivers who deliver the food to the stores, the various clerks in the stores themselves —and there are still more people to enumerate! And all this to give us just one meal—only one of the many aspects which make up an ordinary day. We literally depend on hundreds of thousands of people to help us through daily existence.

Yes, we do depend upon others in so many ways. Long ago the British author, John Donne, wrote that no man is an island. This is a poetic way of saying we are not isolated individuals separated from others.

We are social beings. God has so created us. In so many ways we receive help from others and in turn, it is our duty to give aid to them. It is part of a mature personality to consistently realize our dependence on others and to integrate this basic truth into daily living.

On the other hand, we must not be overly dependent on our brothers and sisters in the human family. To have a morbid need for others is a burden to ourselves and to them alike. A classic example of over-dependence is the hand-wrenching proclamation of one rejected in romantic love, "I cannot go on living without him (or her)!" Of course, this is not objectively true, but so deep is the emotional wound, so deep is the over-dependence, that one person feels it is undeniable. Other common examples of over-dependence are those involving a child toward parents or parents toward a child.

It is no easy task to balance both of these needs—our need for others and our need to be properly independent of them. We will not be mature personalities unless we accomplish this balance to a satisfactory degree. To do so is one of our greatest challenges.

38

Marriage

Marriage is an especially intimate union in which man and woman pledge to share each other's uniqueness in a way which is as awesome as it is beautiful. If a marriage is to be this awesomely beautiful union, the partners must be willing to love authentically. Authentic married love is much more than a warm, romantic glow. This may or may not be present at any given moment of married life, but what should be consistently present is a willingness to give of oneself to the other in order to promote her or his real good. This is true love. This is authentic love. This is the kind of love which prevails in the midst of myriad types of experiences.

All sorts of experiences will mark the path of a married couple as they walk the way of life in a togetherness formed by their mutual love. As their love for each other has initially created this unique togetherness, so will it likewise establish a unified and meaningful existence comprised of happenings and experiences spanning a rich and diversified spectrum of life within the human condition. Their love for each other thus provides a common basis for all kinds of experiences. Ecstatic happiness and deep anguish, such different experiences in one sense, are in another sense similar experiences for husband and wife united in love. The similarity arises because it is the same love which makes the two consistently, tenderly, and beautifully desire to share all experiences. Similiarity thus harmoniously blends with dissimilarity.

This extremely close, unifying love of man and wife is expressed in a most special manner through sexual intercourse. The sexual act is the outward, culminating sign of the partners' pledge to give themselves as completely as possible to each other. It is obvious then, that the sexual act is more satisfying in proportion to each partner's willingness to give of self as much as possible. The woman is usually the more perceptive in this since, compared to the man, it is generally more difficult for her to separate love and sex. If there are, consequently, significant problems with the marriage outside the times of intercourse, this negatively affects the woman's attitude toward the sex act itself. In other words, if her husband is seriously and consistently lacking in giving himself to her in the varied aspects of daily married existence, she intuitively sees the problem with the sexual side of the relationship. Intercourse, ideally the outward sign of the desire of both to give themselves as perfectly as possible to each other in all areas of married existence, certainly suffers when one or both are significantly lacking in this self-gift. A satisfactory sex life is therefore contingent upon the partners' readiness to work effectively at promoting the marriage's growth in all its other aspects. Among other things, this requires a willingness to engage in consistent and meaningful communication.

The marriage union gives a basic orientation to one's stance before God. Ideally, it is a question of approaching God in various ways with another person. This does not mean that a married person does not often approach God singularly. The undeniable truth, however, does remain—married people in many ways stand together before God in love, and together receive God's love.

Married people relate in love not only to God, but to each other, and to their children. They are also meant to relate in love to all others. Here again, marriage is a school of love. Husband and wife, in their mutual sharing of love, grow in their knowledge of how to give and receive love regarding those outside the family circle. They should thus realize their responsibility in contributing to the building of a better world. Man and wife, precisely because of their married love, have their own special responsibility to the secular world. Married love obviously is intimately connected with procreation—with the continuation of the human race, with life upon earth. Life in this world has a quantitative aspect—population numbers—and a qualitative aspect—the kind of life this population lives. There is a connection between the two, because the dignity of the human person requires that the quality of life be fundamentally sound. Consequently, in assuming responsibility to help populate the world, married people are also assuming responsibility to help make this world a more fitting place for their children and others to inhabit.

Our day is witnessing an unusually large number of unhappy and broken marriages. This is a tragedy. It is a tragedy that what is intended to be a uniquely beautiful union often never becomes that, or, once that, disintegrates, and there remain only the ashes of a burnt-out beauty that once was, but now is no more. We mourn these unhappy marriages. We thank God for the happy ones, the beautiful ones, ones which are a testimony to marriage's capacity come what may, to unite husband

and wife in loving and tender concern. The world desperately needs it.

One common thread of advice from couples who have enjoyed many years of marriage is to pray together. Begin that way, and stick to it.

39

Celibacy

Celibacy lived for the sake of the kingdom of God is an important aspect of the Church's life. The fact that our times have witnessed a decrease in the number of celibates does not detract from the fact that celibacy has always been, and is, a powerful force in the life of the Christian community.

Jesus, the founder of Christianity, lived a celibate existence. There have always been those within the Church who have been willing to renounce the great good which is marriage in order to continue this celibate witness.

Committed celibacy is a very meaningful sign pointing to transcendent values. By renouncing one of life's great gifts—marriage—committed celibacy makes a statement to all who would listen that there is something beyond the visible and the tangible. Celibacy is a forceful reminder that there is something beyond marriage and all the other tangible goods associated with life upon this earth. Committed celibacy, then, is a witness to the transcendent dimension of our life of grace in Christ. It is a sign with both present and eschatological dimensions. It points to both the invisible life of grace as lived here below, and to the eschatological fulfillment of that Christ-life in eternity.

The celibate enjoys a certain freedom that the married person does not enjoy. This freedom is another of celibacy's values. A married person must always be aware of his or her obligations to spouse and children. God intends such a person to render a service to Church and world which is compatible with these obligations. Inevitably, this puts certain limitations upon the apostolic—the ministerial—activities of the married person. Celibate freedom, then, is a very significant value in the life of the Church, and the long list of achievements by celibates throughout the history of the Church gives undeniable testimony to this fact.

Celibacy, however, has its own set of restrictions. We must recognize that both celibacy and marriage have limitations attached to them as these vocations make their particular contributions in the work of the Church. They both are life-forms of Christian love, although in different ways. The important thing is for a person to decide which state God intends for him or her. And that state is the one in which the person thinks he or she can best love God and neighbor.

40

Friendship

One of the grandest forms of love we can show for someone is that of friendship. One of its beauties is that it is available to persons of all ages and all vocations. Each of us belongs to a particular state of life and gives and receive love according to the basic dictates of that special vocation. Single and married people in the world, religious, clergy—all of us are meant to love and be loved. Although many of the experiences of love are the same for all, others are indigenous to the particular state of life in question. For example, the celibate cleric is closed off from the experience peculiar to married love just as man and wife, in turn, are not exposed to the pains and joys of celibate love. However, one of the common experiences of love we can all share is that of friendship.

In the course of our daily lives we deal with many people, and some of these we meet rather regularly. We can thus establish amicable relationships with a number of people. We can develop many friends in the process. Deep friendship, however, friendship in the stricter sense of the word, is another matter. For various reasons it seems we establish this type of relationship with only a relatively small number of individuals. Whatever may be the degree and kind of friendship, it is a special gift of God. It indeed plays a treasured role in the Christian life. Christ Himself has shown us this; He, too, had friends, such as Lazarus, Martha, and Mary.

What is friendship, this special, close friendship? It is a mutual self-giving in love. Through this gift of self, friends desire to promote the good of each other. In one's love for a friend, he or she desires that this person becomes everything the friend can become according to God's designs. Through the love of friendship we give ourselves in a very direct, personal, and intimate manner to help achieve this growth.

The desire to give ourself to a friend in such an intimate fashion necessitates that the other also love in return with the love of friendship. You cannot give to another on such a deep level unless that person reciprocally and similarly loves and accepts you as well. The love of friendship, consequently, means a decision to love and be loved in a similar fashion on the part of both.

One of friendship's most distinctive qualities is this mutual acceptance which is given in complete freedom. Friends are radically free to desist loving each other with the love of friendship at any time; yet the fact that they continue to love is one of friendship's glories. Obviously, this is not to say that each and every friendship perenially endures. Sometimes one or both decide for various reasons to end the relationship. Nevertheless, ideal friendship is forever. This demonstrates the necessity of not entering into such a union unless sufficient thought and reflection concerning the responsibilities of friendship have preceded. Full, deep friendship is an important human relationship, and we should treat it in a commensurate fashion.

Friends look at life together and they live life together.

This is why there must be a basic affinity between the two, a basic set of common values and ideals. Otherwise, the close union of friendship does not seem possible. On the other hand, this basic affinity does not exclude all differences. Each person in the friendship is unique and will give his or her individuality to the other with the inevitable differences which distinguish one person from another. These personal differences, properly blended into the unity of friendship, help to enrich the relationship, and each other.

Since friendship is a form of love, it is a life, and as with all life, it must be properly nourished; otherwise, it will wither and die. Each person must realize his or her responsibility in keeping friendship alive and healthy. Notice, we are not saying friends should be morbidly anxious regarding the future of their relationship. We are merely stating that friends, while resting secure in their mutual love, can never afford to take each other for granted.

Friendship is a school of love. Through it God intends to make us Christians who love more sincerely, more deeply, more selflessly.

Since friendship is a school of love, it is evident why it cannot be exclusive. A friendship which makes me less loving toward others needs examination. Although I have a special love for my friends, I cannot neglect a loving concern for all. Jealousy and neglect of duty emanating from a friendship are other indications that not all is right with the relationship. These and other possible negative characteristics should not overly surprise us when they appear, especially if they occur in a minor way. They are simply a sign that we are still learning to love, and that at times we fail to a lesser or greater degree. Negative characteristics of a serious nature, however, should either be eliminated or basically controlled. If there is a serious disorder which is not rectified, the course of action seems obvious. The friendship—or what was a friendship—should be terminated, for the relationship has ceased to be a fundamentally sound form of love.

As always though, we should stress the positive. We should be optimistic about our friendships, confident that with God's grace they will remain what they should be. Christ is the mediator of this grace; it is in His presence and in His assistance that our friendships are to be rooted. In this manner they will flourish and become more beneficial, more profound, and more beautiful.

41

The Acquaintance

There is a definite set of people whom we meet on a fairly regular basis, or at least on numerous times during the year. A few of these people may be friends, but the majority of them are not. People included in this grouping can be quite diverse and might include: our neighbors, the cashier at the supermarket, those with whom we work, those to whom we extend professional service, members of our local Christian community, and those with whom we share membership in various movements and organizations.

People of this type I would like to call acquaintances. I use this term to distinguish them from both the stranger and the friend. We should not think, however, that the term "acquaintance" necessarily implies only a casual relationship. In many instances this will be the case, but in others a significant relationship can be operative. For example, a junior executive can have more than a casual kind of association with the head of a business. He or she may spend much of the working day with this person, share numerous responsible decisions with him or her, and come to develop a sincere admiration for this top executive both as a person and as a business associate. This can hardly be called a casual relationship; yet it can remain a strictly business association without a true friendship ever developing.

We must realize that love shown the acquaintance is a significant implementation of love of neighbor. There are various reasons for this. One of these is that such caring is necessary if ordinary, daily existence is to be reasonably tolerable. For example, if on a particular day the gasoline attendant, the butcher, one of my neighbors, and the dentist's receptionist all treat me in a grumpy fashion, I go to bed that night wondering what was wrong with the human race today. Furthermore, I am not in the best pyschological mood for facing tomorrow.

We must realize that everybody has his or her bad days, and we have to overlook these occasions. In general, however, we rightfully feel that we should be treated in a civil fashion. Obviously, others feel the same way. We also have the obligation to treat acquaintances with a basic kindness and civility.

There is a hierarchy of importance involved in this mutual display of caring and civility which should exist between acquaintances. It is one thing if a certain person in the neighborhood refuses this basic politeness and fails to say hello time after time. It is another matter if a co-worker, with whom one must spend much of the day, manifests a similar coldness. It is one thing if a person feels the sting of racial prejudice inflicted by a stranger. It is another matter if the same act of prejudice comes from people with whom one worships in the Christian community.

Let us resolve to make our full contribution in developing the caring, the kindness, the concern which should exist between acquaintances. Besides our own immediate contribution to the process, our actions can serve as a good example to others and even be a catalyst to their own resolve to act in a similar fashion.

42

The Stranger

A love directed toward strangers may seem to be not all that important. After all, are there not enough other people in our lives, encountered on a rather regular basis, who demand our time and attention? This is certainly true; but on the other hand, love for the stranger should not be made to seem insignificant. Jesus taught that concern for the stranger is indeed a very important aspect of Christian love. He gave us the story of the Good Samaritan, one of Scripture's most inspiring accounts.

If we take time to reflect, it is not all that difficult to comprehend why love for the stranger is an important matter. An encounter with a stranger is usually a one-time occurrence. In rare cases we may meet that person again; however, we really do not expect that to happen.

Because of this factor of the one-time meeting, the love we show the stranger tends to be a very selfless love. Whether the manifestation of love is very ordinary, or heroic, we give it with no realistic expectations of receiving favors from this person in return. These occasions of giving ourselves to strangers have a peculiar power to bring out the purity, the selflessness of our love. We treat the stranger in a proper fashion simply because he or she is a child of God, made in God's image. This is enough for us—this is the decisive factor.

This trait of selfless love, so operative in the gift of self to a stranger, is obviously strengthened each time we exercise it. When we love the stranger we are simultaneously increasing our capacity to love all others more selflessly, including those who are very dear to us.

The specific ways of showing concern for a stranger constitute a long list. The list extends from the very prosaic kindness and courtesy shown a driver in traffic, to the heroic deed of risking one's life to rescue a stranger from a burning house.

The more ordinary ways of showing love for a stranger are important because, among other reasons, they are so constantly available. The more heroic manifestations are also obviously important for a variety of reasons. One of these is that they shock us in a good sense. To see a person risk, and sometimes give, her or his life for a stranger, is a startling experience. It strikingly makes us aware of those recesses of our being—sometimes quite hidden ones—where mediocrity and selfishness lie. Seeing such unselfish manifestations of love toward a stranger, we are prompted to make new beginnings in our own efforts to love more selflessly. Seeing the great reservoirs of human goodness which can become operative in critical situations, we realize anew our own reservoirs of goodness and we resolve, with God's assistance, to further develop it.

The goodness of human nature which prompts heroic deeds on behalf of a stranger is a goodness we all share in our own unique ways. If our own goodness does not have the opportunity to manifest itself through an heroic event, it does provide the opportunity to manifest itself through the extraordinary—or heroic—encounter with the ordinary. Indeed, to love the stranger and others in a consistent fashion among the ordinariness of our lives is its own kind of heroism.

Summarily, we can see that we should not think lightly of the love which is directed at the stranger. We can see that, indeed, the story of the Good Samaritan contains numerous lessons concerning love which affects all of us.

43

The Face of a Child

The face stares out at us from the magazine page. Hunger, loneliness, fear, physical pain—all this is revealed in the tiny features.

The child has not placed these afflictions upon herself. No, forces over which she has no control have put these severe sufferings upon such slight shoulders.

As we look at the picture, what is our reaction? Do we quickly turn to another page to find more pleasant fare? Do we remain basically unmoved by what we see? Do we say others are to blame, and therefore, we have no responsibility toward such children? Or are we sincerely moved? Do we tell ourselves we all have a responsibility to do *something* so that the number of these children will decrease rather than increase?

The picture of the child is there for all of us to see. What picture of ourselves emerges from our particular kind of reaction?

44

Love and Communication

There is a close connection between the gift of self in love and the process of communication. God is the prime example of this. The Father gives Himself to us through the mediatorship of His Son Jesus and accompanying this gift is the divine process of communication. While on earth, Jesus, through word and action, continually revealed the Father, the Father's love for us, and the Father's plan for us. In other words, Jesus was explaining, He was communicating concerning God's gift of love. This process continues as Jesus continues to speak to us through the Spirit.

In our love relationships, there also must be appropriate communication. Between wife and husband, parents and children, friend and friend, fundamental communication must be present if the relationship is to be basically healthy and evolving. Love includes the willingness to communicate.

While communication through words is obviously very important, it is not the only form of communication. Our actions, our total demeanor, are also critical vehicles of communication. As a matter of fact, if one's actions do not basically correspond with one's verbal communication, the words themselves become strongly suspect.

Concerning verbal communication, it is not the quantity of words which is most important—although there is a basic adequacy required in this regard. More critical, though, is the quality of words. Two persons can talk over lengthy periods, but, substantively, not much is being communicated because of the rather superficial level of dialogue.

For true communication to exist between two persons, there is no need for one to speak as much as the other. One person may be of a more talkative nature, the other, of a more reticent bent. As long as each respects the temperament of the other, real communication takes place between such opposites.

The ability to communicate, rather paradoxically, requires the capacity not to speak. In other words, good communication requires that each person be a good listener. Each must sincerely want to hear what the other is saying. One must listen not with a defensive attitude, nor with an attitude which effectively says, "Hurry up so I can begin talking," but rather with a patience which realizes that love includes the desire to try to understand what the other is really feeling and trying to communicate.

Some think that real, ongoing communication in a relationship becomes more difficult over time. Actually, it seems a distinction should be made. In one sense, it seems communication becomes easier as time goes by. The persons know each other better as time progresses, and feel more at ease in the process of communication. On the other hand, if the relationship is truly growing, this means that a deeper love is being shared. Deeper love, in turn, demands a deeper level of communication. In this sense, it seems communication becomes more challenging over the months and years of the relationship.

What about arguments? Does true love, true communication exclude these? I think most would say "no." If the arguments are carried on with loving respect for the other, and with a positive purpose, then argumentation has a place in the ongoing communication process. If the arguments are frequent, however, it seems that something is awry in the relationship and that this very issue—having frequent arguments—should become matter for discussion.

It is not only our more intimate relationships which require proper communication. Our more general ones do also. Proper communication between employer and employee, between teacher and student, between doctor and patient—these are a few examples of the proper dialogue which should be present in our daily existence if needless frustration and other kinds of suffering are to be avoided.

We are followers of the Word made flesh. As the process of communication was so important to the love-mission of Jesus, likewise it is important to us who have been called by Him to aid in the continuation of His work upon earth. Communication has its painful moments, but the joy of a relationship will be wanting if it is not properly present.

45

On Not Being Overly Possessive

One of the difficulties we can encounter in personal relationships is the tendency to be overly possessive of the other. This can happen between marriage partners, friends, parents and children. Being overly possessive is the tendency to place unjust limits on others regarding their activities, particularly those involving other people.

In entering upon a friendship or marriage, a person does not relinquish the right of significant interaction with others. This appears to be so obvious, yet in the concrete affairs of everyday life, the attitude on the part of some put such restraints on others in their lives. Such situations occur frequently.

For example, there is the situation in which a person demands an unreasonable amount of time and attention from a friend. He or she may also become upset because that person has or develops other friendships. To cite another example, some parents place unreasonable demands upon their children in making it difficult for them to choose a marriage partner and begin a life of their own.

This attitude of being overly possessive goes against the dictates of true love. In love for the other, I should want that person to grow in the process of becoming a better person. Through my love, I should help to accomplish this. One way a person grows is to interact with people, and with different types of people. I must, then, allow the loved one to have this opportunity.

We must also remember that an authentic personal relationship, such as a friendship or marriage, is not meant to close in upon itself. For example, two friends in their true love for each other are also learning how better to love others. Each must fight feelings of jealousy and the tendency to be overly possessive—attitudes which restrict growth.

To allow the other his or her proper freedom is not always easy. For some it can even be very painful. We grow by coping with this kind of pain. The situation is different regarding the suffering associated with being overly possessive. This is a pain associated with selfishness and is in itself not growth producing.

Our emotions can partially blind us regarding the evils of being overly possessive. We must take time, therefore, to prayerfully reflect on our personal relationships. Such an exercise is a great help in achieving a proper perspective regarding our interaction with others. Acting upon this perspective, we will experience relationships which are healthier, more joyful, and productive of greater happiness.

46

The Gift of Empathy

One of the marvels of God's creation is the difference between, yet the sameness of, all the billions of human beings who have lived, are now living, and will live in the future. The sameness derives, of course, from the fact that all humans possess the same human nature. The difference emanates from the fact that each of us possesses human nature according to our own individuality, our own uniqueness.

If we reflect upon these truths, we will realize that they constitute a basis for developing a sense of empathy, a much desired characteristic. We all admire those who display a marked ability to empathize, to enter into and share the inner feelings of others, and to manifest an understanding of those feelings.

All of us should and can develop this sense of empathy. One of the best ways to do this is to be in touch with our own inner feelings and experiences. What are some of these? We all know that we want to love and be loved. We all have experienced loneliness. We all have tasted the joy of success and felt the sting of failure. We all have experienced fear and anxiety.

These are some of the human experiences we have all undergone, each according to one's uniqueness. There will be an irreducible difference in these experiences because of this uniqueness; yet the sameness is also undeniable because of our common human nature.

Because of our own experiences, therefore, we are in a position to enter with empathy into the lives of others—to rejoice with them, to grieve with them, to comfort them. Let us not waste the opportunity.

47

Letting Go

He was only eleven years of age. His mother and father had just driven him to school. Very soon after leaving the family car, a school bus, for whatever reason, left the roadway and veered onto the sidewalk. The young boy was struck and killed. A life with so much promise was so suddenly taken in death.

Can we fully comprehend the traumatic shock that must have struck the hearts of this boy's parents? So suddenly, that very significant part of their lives, the loving care of a son, is now no more. No longer will they behold that face, see that smile, hear that familiar voice, touch that hand. So suddenly they must let go of a prized relationship which this life had given them.

The process of letting go that must occur with the death of a loved one is obvious. This process, however, is also called for in a variety of other situations.

The process of letting go manifests itself in various kinds of personal relationships. For example, there comes that time when parents must allow their children to leave home and begin a new kind of life. The parent-child relationship still remains, but both parents and children must let go of that which was appropriate in the earlier stages of the children's existence. A different type of bonding must now be allowed to form. In some cases this is a very difficult process; in others, the transition is less traumatic.

Friendships do not always last. Therefore, we see another kind of relationship which at times occasions the difficult process of letting go. Friendship involves a relationship in which love is mutually given with a very special type of freedom. Other forms of love, such as marriage, can partially depend on such things as juridical ties to preserve the relationship in stormy times. The love of friendship, however, has no such juridical bonds. Friendship is given and received and maintained in complete freedom; yet this complete freedom contains its own kind of possible hurt. A friendship can end with no juridical procedure. When this happens, one or both parties can experience the pain of letting go to a very significant degree.

The necessity of letting go also occurs when a person must leave one job or career and enter a different one. Some are able to achieve this transition with no more than ordinary anxiety. Others can experience very considerable fear when faced with such a prospect.

Letting go occurs when we move from one stage of life to another—from childhood to adolescence, from adolescence to young adulthood, from young adulthood to middle-age, from middle-age to the state of the elderly. These transitions, while producing their own kind of joy, also exact a suffering which for some is very pronounced.

To be sure, properly coping with the process of letting go is not achieved without pain. If we wrongfully cling to what must be left behind, however, we experience a worse suffering which emanates from our immature handling of the situation. We all know which course Jesus wishes us to pursue.

48

Abandonment to God

God gives ultimate meaning to our lives. God reveals to us how the laughter and the tears, the work and the play, the pain and the joy, all fit together. As we live in God, God gathers up what would otherwise be the all-to-fragmented pieces of our lives, and arranges them into a harmonious unity. This unity emanates from our living according to God's plan, a plan embodying a way of existence that leads to an ever greater experience of the true, the good, and the beautiful.

We can put obstacles in the way of God's transforming designs, of God's plan for us. We can at times say "no" to God's initiative. We can refuse to be open to God's tender, loving touch. We can engage in a process of self-enclosure. We can determine to map out our own path to supposed happiness, forgetting that plans for happiness which exclude God are ultimately plans for experiencing frustration and emptiness. Briefly, we can act in an obstinate fashion regarding God's offer of self-communication.

At other times, it is not so much stubbornness which leads us to say "no" to God; it is fear. We realize that the closer we come to God, the more God will ask of us, gently but firmly. We fear the white heat of God's love. Such episodes along the spiritual journey are crucial. If we keep pulling back from the intensity of God's love, if we keep refusing what this love wants to accomplish in us and through us, then we will live on a rather superficial level.

We must strive to overcome whatever attitude prevents us from increasingly giving ourselves over to God. We must realize that progress in the spiritual life is measured by the degree to which we abandon ourselves to God. We must realize that, if we hope to grow spiritually, we must increasingly allow God to direct our lives.

Let us pray, then, for an increase in the spirit of abandonment to God. As we live more according to this attitude, we will experience in greater measure the warmth and security of God's love, this God who is the ground of our being, the goal of our existence, the source of our happiness.

49

God's Presence

Going through Spain, Austria, and Italy by train, I noticed time and again that various small villages had churches which dominated the skyline. These structures commanded attention as the center of existence in these quaint towns. For the inhabitants, these churches stood as symbols of God's dominating presence.

God's presence should also be dominant in our lives. God is the ground of our being, the One in whose image we are made, the One who is the goal of our existence.

Through Christ, God is present to the justified in a special way, and the justified are, indeed, temples of God. Father, Son, and Holy Spirit dwell in them in a most intimate fashion.

Our glorious task is to become increasingly aware of the Divine Presence. Our becoming more aware of God will allow Him to guide us more consistently along the spiritual journey. We become more divinized, more Christlike. More aware of the Divine Presence, we become increasingly sensitive to the way we should think and act. More aware of God within, we work more assiduously to eliminate thoughts and actions inconsistent with the Divine Presence. We determine, with God's grace, to grow in virtue in order to become a more fit dwelling place for the divine.

50

The Spiritual Quest

Throughout this book we have been reflecting on various aspects of the spiritual life. We have seen that in numerous ways we experience both pain and joy as we engage in the spiritual quest. Indeed, unless we properly encounter the pain, we will not experience the joy Jesus wants us to have.

Whatever we have said, or whatever we could say, about the spiritual life centers around Jesus. In St. John's gospel, we read:

> Jesus said to him, "I am the way and the truth and the life. No one comes to the Father except through me." (Jn. 14:6).

The entire effort, then, of one who has entered upon the spiritual quest, is to put on Christ more and more. All authentic efforts in the spiritual life have as their goal the increased emergence of the Christic self within us. We are called upon to grow in the knowledge and love and imitation of Jesus Christ. Our task is to become closer companions of Jesus, this Jesus who, with Mary our Mother at our side, leads us to the Father in the Holy Spirit.

The spiritual quest, then, consists in allowing Jesus

to increasingly take us over—in allowing Him more and more to live in and through us. Allowing Jesus' entrance into our lives has tremendous ramifications. Not only do we achieve our own salvation by committing ourselves to Jesus, but we also assist in the salvation of others.

Some two thousand years ago Jesus walked this earth teaching, healing the sick, extending His mercy and love, forming His Church. These and all His other actions entered into the work of what theologians call objective redemption. We had no part in this redemptive effort of Jesus.

We are now in the phase of what is called subjective redemption, a phase in which the fruits of Christ's objective redemption are distributed over the face of the earth. Each individual is called to salvation. This salvation is Christic; it is the only salvation which exists; it is the one Jesus lived, died, and rose from the dead to accomplish.

According to God's plan, we are called to assist in the work of subjective redemption. According to this plan, Jesus still walks this earth teaching, healing the sick, administering the sacraments, extending His mercy, His love, His concern. He still walks this earth as an irrevocable sign of salvation, as an irrevocable sign that God overwhelmingly loves the world and everlastingly so. Yes, Jesus still walks the earth accomplishing His redemptive work; but now He is present, not through His own humanity, but through our humanities.

We see, then, our great privilege and our great responsibility. Jesus asks us for our humanity, for our human lives, so that He can re-incarnate Himself in us and through us. Of course, it is that kind of re-incarnation which preserves Jesus' identity as well as our own. As a matter of fact, the more we allow Jesus to live in us and through us, the more we become our true selves. The ongoing Christianization of our persons includes the deepened development of our uniqueness.

We can respond to Jesus' request that we allow Him to continue His redemptive work in us in various ways. For instance, we can respond with less than full enthusiasm and live only mediocre Christian existences. We can respond wholeheartedly and tell Jesus that we are completely His, that He can do with us what He wishes. This last response is the one we should expect of ourselves—and we know this deep down where we really live. To go all the way with Jesus is what He deserves, this Jesus who went all the way for us. We must always remember the words of St. Paul and make them our own: *...I live by faith in the Son of God who has loved me and given himself up for me. (Gal. 2:20).*